hook
prod
punch
tuft

DEDICATION

For my beautiful children and grandchildren,
Tamara and Joel, Eloise and Jonah.

Gratitude Dolls. Trish Andersen, 2020
(see page 146).

hook prod punch tuft

Creative Techniques with Fabric and Fibre

Lynne Stein

HERBERT PRESS

LONDON · OXFORD · NEW YORK · NEW DELHI · SYDNEY

HERBERT PRESS
Bloomsbury Publishing Plc
50 Bedford Square, London, WC1B 3DP, UK
29 Earlsfort Terrace, Dublin 2, Ireland

BLOOMSBURY, HERBERT PRESS and the Herbert Press logo are trademarks
of Bloomsbury Publishing Plc

First published in Great Britain in 2023.

A catalogue record for this book is available from the British Library

Library of Congress Cataloguing-in-Publication data has been applied for

ISBN: 978-1-78994-088-6;
eBook 978-1-78994-090-9

1 3 5 7 9 10 8 6 4 2

Designed and typeset by Jerry Goldie Graphic Design.

Printed in China by Toppan Leefung Printing Ltd

To find out more about our authors and books visit
www.bloomsbury.com and sign up for our newsletters.

CONVERSION CHART

Metric		Imperial
2.5 centimetres (cm)	=	1 inch (in)
90 centimetres	=	1 yard (yd)
1 metre (m)	=	39 inches

CONTENTS

1 INTRODUCTION

When the Covid pandemic took hold early on in 2020, severely disrupting, restricting and transforming our lives, we were confronted with the challenge of developing our own particular coping mechanisms and ways of attempting to restore some sense of equilibrium. Many of us were reminded of the basic human need for self-expression. Especially during the periods when we were all locked down, it would have been hard to ignore the extent to which not only other artists, craftspeople and designers, but hobbyists too, seemed to find solace in the act of making. It quickly became apparent on social media platforms such as TikTok, Pinterest, Instagram and YouTube, and on classes being taught on Zoom, that many waking hours were being spent baking sourdough bread, sculpting pots from self-hardening clay and expanding one's vocabulary of embroidery stitches, along with numerous other previously unexplored expressive pursuits.

Creative acts require being in a zone of 'playfulness', allowing ourselves to have fun, experiment and also make mistakes. Science has proven that creative engagement and 'play' have numerous benefits for our health and wellbeing. They have the capacity to calm and comfort, reduce stress and anxiety levels, improve self-esteem and inspire new ideas and ways of thinking. It is no wonder that during a global pandemic, many people around the world sought to engage in these essentially self-healing activities.

On a purely sensual level, there is something very soothing, perhaps even primitive, about the use of many textile tools and implements and the handling of cloth and fibre. The rhythmic, repetitive nature of hand stitching, hooking or punching into cloth is deeply in tune with both mindfulness and the 'slow' movement – their increased popularity being largely due to the widespread experience and health consequences of stress, anxiety and time poverty.

My own practice of more than thirty years and my enthusiasm for the medium of rug hooking comes from a variety of sources, and least of all from any claim to be a talented needlewoman! The medium's simplicity, its folk-art culture, its inventive use of recycling and indeed its social history, with its humble, utilitarian beginnings, all contribute to its persistent appeal. It is largely because of its rich history that this book devotes several pages specifi-cally to the craft; taking a look – past and present – at the many differences in techniques, designs and materials employed across both sides of the Atlantic.

My own art training was in exhibition and display design, and then some years later, as an art therapist. Unlike many other makers and collectors of rag rugs, I have no known personal family history where rag rugs featured in our lives. However, my paternal family were textile traders; my grandmother's shops displaying a sumptuous array of buttons and trimmings. Some of my earliest memories, much to my parents' displeasure, are of unpicking and trying to work out the construction of the candlewick bedspreads which adorned our beds in a style typical of the 1950s.

I have always been challenged and motivated by the notion of creating or refashioning 'something precious out of that which might otherwise have been discarded'. In primitive terms, as a child I would frequently want to investigate the process of combining different found materials and media: ribbons, string, papers, shoe polish, wax and paint. As a design student back in the late 1960s, I was making and selling hand-painted papier maché buttons, brooches and buckles, to appear as fashionable accessories in the pages of glossy magazines.

The fundamental concept of creating marks, pictures, patterns and surfaces from juxtaposed units of looped or tufted colour and texture, is possibly the prime fascination for me as a maker. In this respect, the process of making rag rugs is comparable to mosaic, beadwork, needle punching, collage, pointillism, and even the British tradition of well-dressing, whereby to a degree, found materials also provide some of the interest and inspiration.

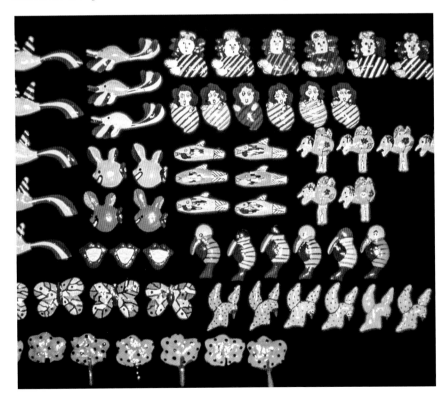

Hand-painted papier-mâché brooches.
Lynne Stein, 1971.
© Lynne Stein

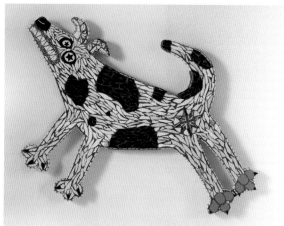

When I was first introduced to the techniques of 'hookie' and 'proggie' at a workshop led by Ali Rhind in the early 1980s, the potential for manipulating fabric and fibre, creating exciting textures, patterns and colour blends, and finding one's own unique and expressive way of working became quickly apparent. The immediacy of the process and the accessibility of tools and materials were also part of the appeal. There was no tedious warping-up of looms or hand-spinning of yarn, and if I was less than satisfied with a particular area, it could be undone and recreated very simply.

Acquiring the necessary tools for this craft involves little expense. Rummaging around thrift stores and charity shops for fabrics is most definitely part of the preliminary fun. The basic methods and techniques of rag rugging are easily learnt, providing scope for creating a broad range of both decorative and functional items: cushions and corsages, hangings and handbags. The possibilities for collaborative making – whether as a family, a group of friends,

Above left: *Wentworth Chair* (detail). Early twenty-first century. Mosaic.
© Candace Bahouth

Top: *Hatching Rocks*. NanC Meinhardt, 2009. 25 × 36 cm (10 × 14 in). Embroidered, free-form right-angle weave. Glass seed beads.
© NanC Meinhardt

Above: *Hot Dog* (Pharma's Market). Cleo Mussi, 2009. 80 × 52 cm (31½ × 20½ in). Mosaic. Recycled crockery.
Photo: Peter J. Stone

or as a school or community project – are diverse. In my many projects over the years, with different groups of people, young and old, it is obvious to me that rag rugging, rather like the traditional quilting bee, is socially as well as creatively therapeutic, offering the opportunity to participate on so many levels. This might simply involve contributions of cast-off clothing or the provision of anecdotal information to inform the design of a wall hanging. As well as being enjoyed by children, it can be a beautiful translator of their artwork; and part of its appeal for an older generation undoubtedly lies in the memories triggered. Aesthetically, the medium often seems to be enriched by its collaborative nature.

Top: *DZESI II*. El Anatsui, 2006. 303 × 463 cm (121 × 185 in). Aluminium bottle caps, copper wire.
© El Anatsui

The density and compactness of the looped or tufted pile produce a sturdy and durable finished textile, and as long as this is not exposed constantly to harsh sunlight, the colours retain their vibrancy. I have been told many stories of stair runners made during the 1930s and earlier, which are still well and truly intact despite having been subjected to phenomenal wear and tear.

The terminology attached to the tools and methods of rug making are, to some extent, geographically dependent. In County Durham, for instance, the word 'proggie' would replace 'probby', used in Berwick-upon-Tweed, or 'peggy'

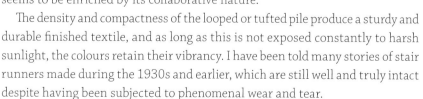

Above: Well-dressing. Eyam, Derbyshire.
© Lynne Stein

Above left: Lynne Stein with Simonstone Primary School and Eleanor Palmer (detail). Gawthorpe Hall residency, 2000.
© Lynne Stein

Above right: An ongoing project involving people with visual impairment, 2009. © Heather Ritchie/ Rug Aid

Left: *Las Rancheritas Rug Hook Project, Oralia Mermaid*, 2010. 92 × 81 cm (36 × 32 in). Hooked wool and polar fleece.
© Charlotte Bell

and 'tabby' in other regions. All indicate the method of pushing short strips of mostly recycled fabric through the reverse of a hessian backing cloth to achieve a soft, thick, shaggy pile. Hooking and prodding involve the use of different tools, and achieve different surfaces. As basic textile processes, however, they combine and are compatible with other materials and ways of working. Some of my projects will, I hope, encourage you to explore these possibilities.

Rag rugs, like patchwork quilts, were born out of necessity, as a way of providing some domestic warmth to an otherwise cold stone floor. Increased ecological awareness, the fashion for wooden and stone floors to replace wall-to-

Left: *The Women of Santiago Atitlán.* Juana Yolanda Charnel Ajú. Chuacruz, Sololá, Guatemala. © Multicolores, Guatemala

Below: *Bar-B-Que.* Ronald Veasey, Creative Growth Art Center, 1990. 90 × 106 cm (35 × 42 in). Hooked wool. © Ronald Veasey

wall carpets, and a certain revived interest in 'home crafts' and domesticity, all contribute towards the resurgence in the relevance and popularity of rag rugs within the lands of their origins and beyond. Guilds and groups continue to grow and thrive on both sides of the Atlantic. Museums and galleries exhibit and introduce the work of both established and lesser-known makers. Magazines, newsletters, blogs and forums are published, always with something new to say.

Socially and economically beneficial projects and inspiring innovations have taken place in various parts of the world, from Heather Ritchie's Rug Aid in the Gambia, Mielie in South Africa, Las Rancheritas in Mexico and Multicolores in Guatemala, to the hand-hooked woollen textiles being made by adults with developmental disabilities at the Creative Growth Art Center in California. The Boucherouite rugs made by Moroccan Berber tribal women would be hard to surpass as a stunning example of the links between necessity and inventiveness. The term *bu sherwit* means a scrap or piece torn from pre-used clothing. Synthetic fibres, including lurex, nylon and plastic, now provide the weft materials and the means of continuing a tradition and livelihood from rug making, since widespread drought in the 1980s caused a devastating scarcity of wool.

Rag rugging as a medium frequently appeals to painters, stitchers, graphic artists and sculptors alike for its versatility and its capacity for enhancing creativity, renewing colour theories and exploring textile behaviours. In more recent times, the ever-increasing popularity and use of latch hooks, punch needles and even tufting guns would have been difficult to ignore. Perhaps it was the proliferation of images of textile creations on social media that initially whet my appetite. I too was encouraged to experiment and widen my own vocabulary of tools and techniques, mixing, matching and often documenting the results. There is no reason why some projects should be limited by the use of a singular tool and texture; the stitched scribbles wall hanging project on page 113 exemplifies the possibilities of combining different processes.

In much of the work of other artists and makers included in this book,

Above left: Boucherouite rug, late twentieth century. 122 × 127 cm (48 × 50 in). Knotted with a symmetrical knot pile. Rag and lurex. © Gebhart Blazek/ courtesy berber-arts.com

Above: *Totems*. Ali Rhind, 1996 (part of a larger installation). Prodded wool. Photo: David Lawson

there is an obvious joy in the use, potential and sometimes recent discovery of their medium, whether that involves hand-hooked methods to construct three-dimensional works, a variety of tools and vibrantly coloured woollen yarns to produce sumptuous sculptural surfaces, or a punch needle to create complex illustrative works. It seems that as well as in their use of colour, one of the most seductive qualities common to all these processes is the capacity for tactility and sensory touch.

With a somewhat 'maverick' approach in my own making, it is my hope that this book and the different projects and processes described within it might transmit my love of experimentation and 'playfulness', and will introduce new ideas, techniques, ways of working and the encouragement to push boundaries. I hope in some cases that it might also demonstrate the wide application for and within a diverse range of settings, including schools, libraries, hospitals and residential homes for the elderly. Perhaps you are already 'addicted' and I am preaching to the converted; but if you are a newcomer to any, or indeed all of the processes, I hope that they will provide you with many satisfying hours of making and give you pleasing results.

Coral Garden. Vanessa Barragão. Mixed techniques. Recycled materials, repurposed factory waste yarn.
© Studio Vanessa Barragão: Textile Art & Design Studio

2 RAG RUGS: A Brief History

The technique of constructing a textile by manipulating loops or tufts through a woven foundation is a very old one; it probably precedes the technique of knotted pile, dating back to ancient Coptic textiles, around 2000 BC, in Egypt. The first examples of rugs were evident in Danish Bronze Age graves, and somewhat later in Viking and Celtic tombs. Ann Macbeth, Head of Embroidery at Glasgow School of Art from 1911 to 1920, wrote that the methods were introduced to the Scots by the Vikings. Their construction was of raw fleece loops, which emulated the feel and warmth of sheepskin, and would have been used mostly for bed coverings, replacing the earlier skins and furs. The Shetland Islands were part of Norway until the fifteenth century, and similar textile methods were evident here until this time. The Viking influence is still evident in Scotland and Northern England, in terms of language, patterns and designs.

Rag rugs made from fabric remnants are in fact common to several cultures, and the forerunners and influences, in terms of looped pile, include ropework and the textile traditions of sailors and their wives, medieval tambour work, and possibly, the Spanish Alpujarra peasant folk-art rugs, from the fifteenth to nineteenth century.

The oldest surviving rag rug in Britain apparently used army uniforms, worn in the Battle of Waterloo in 1815. The heyday of rag-rug making in the UK, however, was in the late nineteenth and early twentieth century. Beyond the Industrial Revolution, the availability of cheaper mass-produced fabrics and clothing, access to mill remnants and thrums for 'rags', and the advent of jute hessian from India in the 1850s, were certainly contributing factors to continued practice of the craft. Sacks, which had contained flour, sugar, potatoes and coffee, were also imported from India and could occasionally be coaxed from a friendly grocer. From the early twentieth century, hessian or burlap could be purchased quite cheaply by the yard, and ready-printed designs had also become more affordable.

The reason for the relative lack of documentation of rag-rug making in the British Isles is partly due to the fact that, in its day, it was undervalued as a craft. There is a scarcity of examples in museum collections because most rugs were worn through before making it this far. Often having been worked in the autumn months to brighten the Christmas hearth, they would gradually, during

Above: Unknown maker, 1930s–40s. 145 × 77 cm (57 × 30 in). Courtesy: Maureen Morano. © Robbie Wolfson

Left: *Tiger Rug*. Unknown maker, 1960s, Newcastle area. 106 × 76 cm (42 × 30 in). Courtesy: Maureen Morano. © Robbie Wolfson

the course of the year, be demoted, via the scullery, eventually reaching the 'privy' or the compost heap outside!

It is easy to romanticise the craft as practised then, and to forget the blistered fingers, the cutting out of seams and other preparatory tasks, not to mention the sheer weight of the work as it progressed. The origins of rag-rug making were probably essentially European, but in Britain, unlike North America and Scandinavia, it was simply a folk art born of necessity and rooted in poverty, and as much an activity of everyday life as brewing tea and darning socks.

Particularly in mining communities, the craft often involved the entire family, demanding only minimal skills and negligible cost. Materials were swapped and bartered amongst neighbours, home-made toffees were passed around, and help in finishing a rug could be exchanged for a simple meal and was occasionally even the exchange mechanism for rent. The men would often draw the design of a rug with a fire-charred stick, and usually made the rug frames, which were sometimes shared amongst an entire street. Frames were used, especially in Scotland and Northern England, to speed up the work; they would be the focal point of the living room, occupying most of the available space and most of the family's attention! Tools might be fashioned from nails, keys, whale bones, sheep's horns and carved parasol handles. Sometimes they were made at the local blacksmith, foundry or shipyard. In the 1920s and 1930s, family cohesion was expressed in the making of a 'clippie' mat to adorn the hearth, which took pride of place in the home. Children were often only allowed out to play once their quota of 'hookie' or 'proggie' pieces had been cut!

Recycled soft furnishing scraps, black wool on hessian. Unknown maker, nineteenth century. A common motif within the rugs of fishing communities, the diamond was believed to avert the evil eye. Scottish Fisheries Museum. Donated by Mrs Doig, Cellardyke, 1970s.
Photo: Vicky Brown

There is a strong history of making rag rugs from Motherwell to Morecambe Bay, and particularly in Tyneside, but there is evidence of the craft in most parts of the UK, especially in mining, seafaring and rural farming communities. The only real differences are the local terms for tools and techniques, such as 'tabbie', 'proggie' and 'bodger'. Methods and traditions only differed slightly according to region and circumstances, such as the use in fishing communities of trawlermen's jersey wool for the 'rags' and kipper dyes to produce beautiful shades of brown and orange. Since the usual source of materials for a rug was a worn-out tweed jacket or a pair of old woollen breeches (no item of family clothing being discarded), colours were often earthy and sombre. Red material, occasionally salvaged from a flannel petticoat or a military uniform, was often coveted and considered to have protective powers, and used 'to ward away the devil, should he look down the chimney'.

In mining families particularly, bed coverings made for the winter were later used as 'summer mats', while in many fishing communities, everyday mats were removed to make room for the Sunday mat. In some areas, the tradition of 'rolling in the new mat' was a ritualised celebration, undertaken by the youngest child of the household.

Although there was a lull in making after the First World War, rag rugs were made well into the 1930s, particularly in more economically depressed areas. By the Second World War, with its 'make-do-and-mend' imperative, the availability of synthetic dyes and different materials had increased, and other methods and techniques such as dyeing, knitting and crochet were occasionally incorporated into rugs.

The prodded or pegged rug was common in the north east and the south of England, creating simple but utilitarian rugs for warmth. These were also made in Scotland and the north west. 'Hookies' and 'clippies' (terms to distinguish between looped and tufted rug pile) were popular, the loops sometimes being sheared to give a softer, more even texture. Until the 1960s, patterns were generally simple, often employing household crockery, brown paper or cardboard cut-outs as templates for geometric motifs or scalloped borders. Cumbrian rugs often featured a central lozenge shape, surrounded by an area of random mixed colours, known as 'mizzy-mazzy', and dark borders, which were frequently made from stockings. The designs of this region gradually became more figurative and pictorial, often featuring animals such as cows, bulls and horses. 'Crazy paving' designs influenced by patchwork quilts were also popular. For several decades after the war, the craft virtually disappeared, due to negative associations with poverty and affordable options for floor coverings, including wall-to-wall carpet.

In the early 1920s, soon after they were married, the artists Winifred and Ben Nicholson settled in Cumberland, close to Winifred's childhood home, and were impressed by the charming and primitive designs of rag rugs made by their neighbours. Amongst them, Margaret Warwick and her daughters, Janet Heap and Mary Bewick, created rugs which were regarded as 'folk art' and attracted collectors. In the 1960s, after divorcing, Winifred, on whom the resourcefulness of the Cumbrian lifestyle had left an enduring impression, was approached by Nancy Powell, another enthusiastic craftsperson, to engender local interest

Dyed woollen fabric scraps tufted onto a knitted string-and-hessian base. Elizabeth Nunn, Sydney, Australia, *circa* 1939. The maker moved to Australia from Britain in 1901, and worked as a corsetiere in a large Sydney department store, where many of the rug's offcuts were obtained. Donated by and © Grace Flinn. Collection: Powerhouse Museum, Sydney. Photo: Jean-François Lazarone

in the craft. With the help of her son Jake, and her grandchildren, approximately 180 rugs were designed. Many of these were made by Mrs Davidson from Bewcastle and Florence Williams. Living next door to Otterburn Mill at Warwick Bridge, a popular source for fabric offcuts, Miss Williams, noted for her vibrant palette, would often search through mill clippings to obtain just the right colours for the rugs.

In the 1970s, in nearby Lanercost, artists Audrey and Denis Barker, with the intention of improving design standards, involved local makers such as Florence Williams in the execution and interpretation of their designs. Like Winifred Nicholson, they encouraged all makers to express their individuality in terms of colour and occasional compositional adjustments.

Crafts such as rug making and quilting were taken by emigrants to North America, particularly to maritime areas such as Maine and New England, New Brunswick, Nova Scotia, Prince Edward Island, Quebec, Newfoundland and Labrador. By the end of the nineteenth century, rugs were made all over North America.

Fishing and farming were common ways of life during this time, and families faced harsh and austere conditions and severe, lengthy winters. Thrift and resourcefulness were essential in furnishing their humble homes. Given that all the preliminary processes for clothing the family and furnishing the home, such as weaving, spinning and dyeing, were hugely labour-intensive, every scrap of fabric was cherished and eventually transformed into a patchwork quilt or a hooked rug. These textile crafts provided a vehicle for creativity, introducing warmth and cheer into an otherwise dismal and unwelcoming domestic environment.

Imported carpets – even those which were factory-made by the 1820s – were prohibitively expensive. Floor coverings had often consisted merely of

Two Cats by the Fire. Margaret Warwick, *circa* 1923. 58 × 124 cm (23 × 49 in). Margaret Warwick was Winifred Nicholson's next-door neighbour, and the work features in one of Ben Nicholson's drawings from this era. Tullie House Museum and Art Gallery Trust. Photo: Guy Paule

Above: Hooked rug. Florence Williams, 1960s. The tweeds and scallops in the border, which so distinguish her work, were obtained from Otterburn Mill, where she was employed. Courtesy Maureen Morano. © Robbie Wolfson.

Below: *Peacock*. Winifred Nicholson, *circa* 1970. 84 × 138 cm (33 × 54 in). Hooked by Florence Williams. Inspired by a Ravenna mosaic of a similar theme, colour and composition. Courtesy of Tullie House Museum and Art Gallery Trust. Photo: Guy Paule.

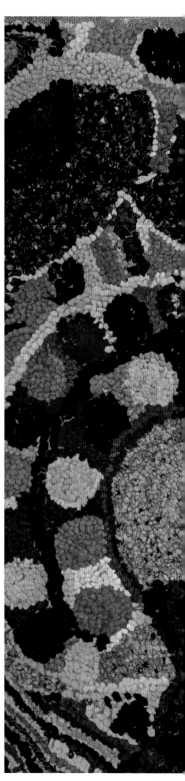

Above: Unknown maker. Mid-twentieth century. 20 × 86 cm (47 × 34 in). Courtesy Maureen Morano. © Robbie Wolfson

Below: *General George Washington.* Unknown maker, *circa* 1880. 145 × 102 cm (57 × 40 in). Hooked wool and wool jersey. Political and patriotic themes feature frequently in American hooked rugs of the period. © Just Folk, California

Above: Hooked rug. Magdalena Briner Eby. Courtesy of the Historical Society of Perry County.
Photo: Jane Hoover

grease-absorbing sand, swept into swirls, chevron and herringbone patterns. Amongst wealthier families, floors were decorated with stencilling and painted floorcloths. Until the 1830s, the earliest 'ruggs' or 'ryiiys', with their long Scandinavian history, were actually bed coverings, and add meaning to the saying, 'snug as a bug in a rug'! By the mid-nineteenth century, imported Indian jute hessian, known as burlap, provided an efficient and affordable backing cloth. This changed the course of rug making. Hooking, because of its durability and defined imagery, now superseded such earlier techniques as braiding, shirring, yarn sewing, pulled 'shag mats' and appliquéd 'dollar mats'. Designs for the earliest hooked rugs were drawn freehand, and reflected the maker's domestic environment, including farmstead animals, flowers and fruit. Outer edges were often given linear borders, or adorned with scallops, scrolls and floral forms. Ships, shells and other depictions of marine life appeared in the rug designs of sailors' wives, and would be surrounded by backgrounds of contrasting colour and texture. Patriotic themes also adorned some rugs, bearing the eagle or American flag, and slogans or words such as 'union'. During the nineteenth century, the Shakers, who were skilled designers and craftspeople, developed their own style. Their rugs, which could be sold for seventy cents per square foot, display evidence of the importance they placed upon function, aesthetics and thrift.

By the end of the nineteenth century, cheaper carpets became available, and home rug making declined. However, as in Britain, the American Arts and Crafts movement grew out of a dissatisfaction with mass production, and a desire to preserve traditional skills. Design ideas came from numerous sources, including geometric shapes, overlapping clamshells, traditional patchwork quilts or more elaborate carpet patterns in catalogues. Animals on metal weathervanes, as well as stencils and domestic crockery, were used as templates, and paintings and furniture carvings were copied. Narrative scenes recorded family events, and were occasionally accompanied by humorous phrases or wise sayings. As in Britain, one of the simplest but most effective designs was a mixture of multi-coloured fabrics in a random manner, known in America as 'hit or miss'. Until the 1860s, when chemical dyes became available (some 700 by 1902), a wide but subtle colour palette could be obtained from leaves, berries, plants and vegetables, such as brazilwood, walnut, hickory, sumac, elderberry, cochineal and onion skins. Rugs with a relief surface from sculpted pile, perhaps depicting a floral wreath, animal or basket of fruit, became known as Waldoboro rugs, from the town of their origin in Maine.

Attempts were being made to make the craft of rug making more accessible. The first printed rug designs appeared in the 1850s. In the 1860s, Edward Sands Frost, a tinware pedlar from Maine, while watching his wife's rug hooking attempts with poor tools and designs, set about creating stencils for printing made from old copper boilers. In 1881 Ebenezer Ross patented the Novelty Rug Machine, which, resembling a shuttle hook, helped to speed up the hooking process. Towards the end of the century, mail-order firms such as Sears Roebuck and Montgomery Ward featured patterns for printed designs in their catalogues, many of which were copies of both Frost and Ross. While it could be said that a 'painting by numbers' approach might have stifled creativity, it certainly popularised the craft, and many makers adapted the designs and introduced colourways according to their own taste. Helen Rickey Albee was one of the first during the Arts and Crafts movement to set up a cottage

Grenfell mat. *Circa* 1970s. 41 × 30 cm (16 × 12 in). Finely hooked wool on hessian. © Anne and Malvin Flynn

industry in New Hampshire, outsourcing work to the local farmers' wives. In the early part of the twentieth century, several other cottage industries followed, many designs being inspired by Native American designs and Navajo blankets, and all enabling the rug makers to earn an extra income.

With the Colonial Revival style, interest in the early American crafts increased. During the Arts and Crafts movement, exhibitions showcasing the rugs were more frequent and provided continuing sales outlets for cottage industries such as the Subbekashe Rug Industry, at the beginning of the twentieth century. Country folk erected stalls along the roadside or sold their work from home.

From the 1920s, with increasing mobility and car ownership, collectors and interior decorators would travel considerable distances to New England and Canada in search of an 'antique'; a rare hooked rug, displaying all the patience, skill and often humour of its maker. During the 1940s, auction sales of rugs took place, particularly in New York.

In 1892, William Grenfell, an English doctor, was sent as a missionary to deep-sea fishermen on the Canadian coast of Labrador. Although he found appalling conditions – extreme poverty, lack of hygiene and consequent sickness – he was charmed by both the place and the people and decided the following year to dedicate his life to improving theirs, by setting up the Grenfell Mission. Hospitals, schools and industries were established, as was the Mission boat, offering mobile medical help.

Although early French influence is apparent, Grenfell regarded the tradition of rug hooking as having probably been brought to the Canadian maritime provinces by Scottish and Cornish settlers, who had learnt the craft as children. Although the local women were obviously familiar with the techniques and had great expertise in making, they mainly used dowdy old clothes for fabrics, and he was disappointed by the lack of design and colour sense in their work. Acknowledging rug making as a viable means of earning money, and the necessity of raising standards to meet the requirements of wealthy collectors in the US and Canada, he engaged Miss Jesse Luther, an occupational therapist and talented designer, to supervise the work of up to 2,000 women per year. Designs were often figurative, displaying local animals such as reindeer and beavers, and maritime themes.

Later Rhoda Dawson, whose designs were rather more modern and abstract, took over. In the 1930s and 1940s, responding to the slogan, 'when your stocking starts to run, let it run to Labrador', supporters of the Mission sent silk and rayon stockings to replace the flannelette that had been formerly used for the mats. Sales outlets were established in Canada, along the eastern seaboard, Philadelphia, Vermont and as far away as England.

As demand from collectors in America continued to grow, original designs were still being executed well into the twentieth century. At the end of the nineteenth century, on Cape Breton Island, Nova Scotia, an artist by the name of Lillian Burke was engaged by the wife of Alexander Graham Bell to set up the Chéticamp hooked rug industry. Again, she noted the obvious potential amongst local makers, but was unimpressed by their choice of colours, and pledged to improve design standards. Demand frequently called for large-scale rugs, with several women working together on one piece for months at a time. Design inspiration occasionally came from museum collections of paintings and textiles. Earnings from rug making sometimes constituted a family's entire income.

Crucifixion. Élizabeth LeFort , 1964. 168 × 300 cm (66 × 120 in). Including 510 hand-dyed colours, this painterly work took 187 days to hook. Courtesy of La Société Saint-Pierre, Chéticamp.

Very much a winter occupation, when fishing and farming were less busy, rug making was equally well-established in Newfoundland and Nova Scotia, and there are similarities between these and the rugs from New England, although the Americans normally used pure wool rather than a mixture of materials.

Hooked T-shirt fabrics by Mielie, a business initiative in Capetown creating bags and homeware products. Masterminded by Adri Schutz, it provides employment for women, allowing them to work from home. © Mielie

The earlier examples, made by the French settlers in Nova Scotia and Cape Breton Island, were sheared yarn-sewn rugs, creating an undulating, sculptural pile, distinguishing the central motif from its background and bearing some resemblance to the Waldoboro rugs. The craft was also evident in Quebec and Ontario, where the tradition seems to have survived for centuries, with influences including tambour and ecclesiastical embroidery. By 1900, 'stamped mats' were available here. Designs were also stabbed with a needle, through the outline of a shape onto thick brown paper, to be cut into a template.

Debate about the origins of rag rugs, both geographically and chronologically, continues. It is clear that as well as having been a thrift craft, at times it has also afforded makers the opportunity of creating powerful and personal visual statements. Like previous cottage industries on both sides of the Atlantic, relatively new initiatives, which also aim to empower and improve the lives of rug makers and their families, emerge continually in different parts of the world. Today, rag rugs, as well as carrying the creative expression of the maker, resonate with current ecological concerns, and the desire once more to conserve, recycle and repurpose.

3 MATERIALS, TOOLS AND EQUIPMENT

Hooking and prodding tools

One of the distinct advantages of traditional rag-rug making is that it is not expensive to get started. As a beginner, you only need very basic equipment: a simple frame, backing cloth, scissors, a rug hook, a prodder and a range of predominantly recycled materials. However, the other equipment described in this chapter may either be selected as alternatives for making any number of textile projects, or indeed be combined with each other as a means for creating exciting textural surfaces.

Materials

Your choice of fabrics will very much depend upon your project. If you are planning a rug or mat for the floor, you will need to consider such factors as shrink and dye resistance, washability and general durability. Certain synthetic fibres are extremely hard-wearing. However, if you are aiming for something more decorative and pictorial, such as a wall hanging or even a cushion, the possibilities are almost limitless.

Medium-weight woollen fabrics and flannels can be suitable and will take dyes well, but they are also relatively expensive. Car-boot sales, charity shops, cast-offs and occasionally fabric websites can all provide rewarding and inexpensive sources for developing your range of colours, weights and textures. Scarves, shawls and wraps, as well as certain larger items of clothing, can prove to be excellent finds. Keepsake and 'rite of passage' garments such as ties, wedding dresses and christening robes might contribute to a very personal heirloom piece.

As well as judging a fabric on its suitability for the job, you should take its aesthetic appearance into consideration. Available fabrics might include: crimplene, velour, organza, net, satin, silk, polyester, towelling, plastic, paper, ribbon, lurex, nylon, soft and supple leather and suede, sweet wrappers, cotton, wool, lace, fleece, knitwear and linen. As well as dyed and natural unspun fleece, a wide range of yarns can also be introduced, such as mohair, rug and knitting wool, chenille, embroidery and sari silk, linen and metallic thread, slub, space-dyed and novelty yarns.

When trying to estimate the amount of fabric required for your strips, roughly fold the fabric in four over the area of the design to be worked. However, I personally find that running out of a certain fabric is rarely a disaster, as part of the medium's charm and richness is the blending of closely related tones and textures.

Dyeing fabrics for a particular project is generally less common in the UK, where there seems to be less concern for intricate tonal gradations and hyperrealism.

All fabrics should be washed before use, and any buttons, pockets, waistbands, collars, cuffs, zips and facings removed. However, like torn or frayed edges, stitched and overlocked fabrics can provide textural interest in your work. You will find it helpful eventually to sort your fabrics into colours and store them in transparent plastic bags or stacking boxes.

A selection of the author's fabrics, fibres, scoobies, ribbons, braids and other embellishment artefacts.
© Lynne Stein

Backing cloths

The prime considerations for selecting the appropriate backing cloth or foundation fabric are that the weave should be sufficiently open and even, and easy to manipulate with your tools. The fabric should be non-stretch, stable and durable. This might include linen, monks cloth, wide-mesh rug canvas and even certain plastic garden meshes, in the case of an exterior project. However, you might also wish to try knitted or crocheted fabrics, which can result in quite a warm and substantial fabric.

Rug canvas is likely to dictate a somewhat more linear and geometric approach. Traditionally, the backing cloth for a rug would have been hessian or burlap. This is still commonly used, and generally should be bought as best quality 280 g (10 oz) weight or finer, depending upon the project. It is normally sold in 90 and 120 cm (3 and 4 ft) widths. If using recycled sacks, it is important that there are no holes or flaws in the weave, which could spoil your work.

Frames

A frame will achieve and maintain tautness in your backing cloth, making hooking far easier. It must allow for periodically viewing the textile in progress, and its size must allow you to reach the centre of your work easily. To begin with, you may just want to try a simple, inexpensive wooden canvas stretcher. These are available in various sizes, and your work can be moved along the frame as a section is completed. As you progress, you may find it handy to have a variety of frames in different shapes and sizes, depending on your particular project.

The author at work in her studio. © Lynne Stein. Photo: Robbie Wolfson

Quilting hoops, particularly when worked with fine yarns and thinly cut strips of material, can be ideal for jewellery and small projects. Square pine frames can be quickly assembled and taken apart, and can be propped up against either a table or the back of a chair. There are a variety of lap and floor frames, and combinations of both, which use carding strips or gripper rods along each side to secure the backing cloth. These have the advantage of freeing your hands and will swivel and rotate for ease. An adjustable rolling frame can be particularly useful if embarking on a sizeable piece of work or a collaborative project. This is comparable to a traditional rug or quilting frame, with carpet webbing tacked along the two long sides, onto which the backing cloth can be stitched. Two movable slats slide through these bars, with pegs for tensioning, and can be released and reassembled to expose the next part of the design. The frame can be set up on trestles or tabletops of the same height.

Rug hooks

The specific function of the type of hook you choose will be important, as will its size and feel for comfort. A smooth, turned yew rug hook handle, for instance, can be very comforting and therapeutic to use. With luck, old rug hooks can occasionally be found in junk shops or online.

The standard 'primitive' rug hook is appropriate for executing the majority of the projects in this book. You may also find an extra-fine pencil hook useful for working with yarns and very fine fabric strips on smaller scale projects.

Spring-clip hooks or bodgers can be used without a frame and create a thick shaggy surface, comparable to pegged or prodded rugs. Speed hooks, shuttle hooks and punch needles can be useful tools, creating a 'walking' motion across the reverse side of the backing cloth, to produce a row of loops on the other side. Their slight limitations might include having less flexibility with the width of your rag strip, and the need to constantly review your work on the opposite or right side.

The locker needle combines a wide eye at one end and a hook at the other. It pulls yarn through the loops created and provides an extra secure surface, holding the loops fast and giving a slightly woven appearance. Different sizes are available for different scales of work.

Prodders

Historically, these were fashioned from any number of available items, from parasol handles to clothes pegs and whale bones, the crucial factor being the smooth point, made for pushing the fabric through a space in the backing cloth. Once again, a smooth bulbous-handled prodder can make for more comfort, and various types are available, made from both wood and metal.

Dolly pegs, with one side sawn off and the other carved to a smooth point, can also be used. Even a pencil or crayon can be used when working with a class of young children.

Above: Ali Rhind's varied collection of prodders.
Photo: Jane Frazer

OTHER USEFUL EQUIPMENT

- Sewing machine, needles, pins, bodkins, kilt and safety pins, string, thread
- Iron and pressing cloth, old towels
- Drawing pins, hammer, staple gun and staples, staple remover
- Compass, stiff card or cereal boxes for templates
- Graph paper, tracing paper, non-stick baking parchment, carbon paper, brown paper, drawing paper, clear acetate
- Indelible thick and thin marker pens in various colours, tailor's chalk, transfer pencil, masking tape
- Ruler, metal yardstick, tape measure
- Pair of trestles, G-clamps
- Latex carpet adhesive, metal or plastic spreader, all-purpose glue
- Crochet hook, knitting needles, felting needles, felting mat or sponge
- Heat gun
- Flexible wire, scoobies
- Beads, buttons, glass nuggets, pom-poms, shisha mirrors, junk jewellery, etc.

Right: Tools and equipment for a range of projects of different sizes and techniques.
© Lynne Stein

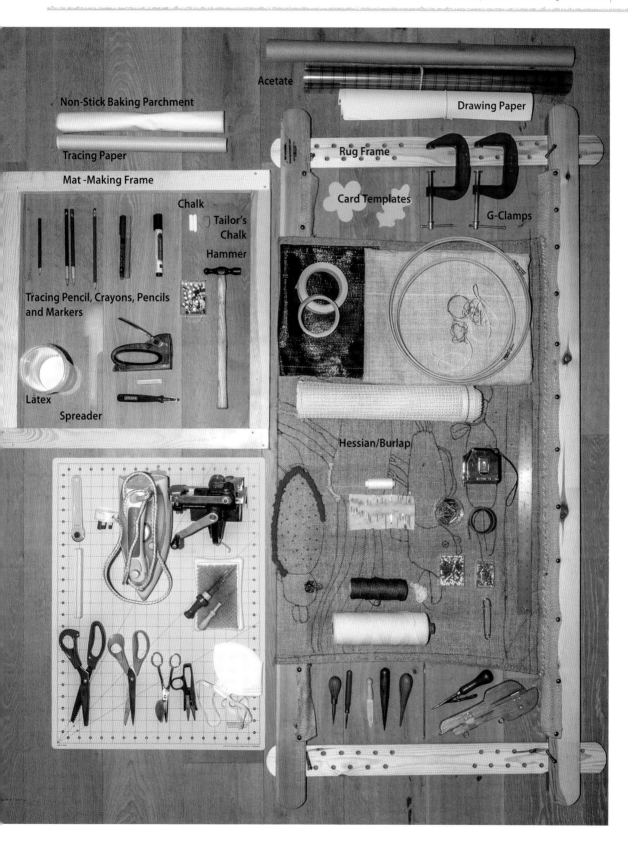

Acetate

Non-Stick Baking Parchment

Drawing Paper

Tracing Paper

Rug Frame

Mat -Making Frame

Card Templates

Chalk

Tailor's Chalk

G-Clamps

Hammer

Tracing Pencil, Crayons, Pencils and Markers

Latex

Spreader

Hessian/Burlap

Cutting tools

Generally, my preference is simply for a range of scissors of different sizes. I use long-bladed shears, embroidery scissors, napping shears with offset handles, and sharp scissors with shorter blades or thread snips for trimming off stray ends of threads and fabric and fine detailed work, such as fleece and yarn sculpting. Pinking shears can be useful for cutting pieces of fabric for prodding, particularly with sturdy materials like felt, and for creating extra texture. Many fabrics such as cotton and polyester can be snipped and torn along their grain, sometimes producing an attractive frayed edge.

You may find a rotary cutter and cutting board helpful if you have available work surface, as these will help to produce straight and even strips of fabric.

A machine cutter, which can be clamped onto a table, can also be a useful piece of equipment. However, these are quite expensive and are more easily available in the US. They do not handle man-made and flimsy fabrics such as Crimplene and nylon well, and although they allow different cutting widths, changing the blades to achieve this is time-consuming.

A sewing machine might come in handy for sewing hems, attaching linings and joining rag-rug panels. A variety of needles are useful for various tasks, from stitching with rag strips to attaching hessian onto the webbing of a rug frame. If you are doing any plaiting or braiding, you will need large kilt pins to anchor your fabric as you work.

An iron will be useful for transferring designs onto your hessian, and also for heat-bonding processes, for which you will also need towels and non-stick baking parchment. Acetate sheets, rulers and yardsticks can also be useful aids for scaling and transferring designs. Tailor's chalk is helpful, particularly if you are a little nervous about drawing, to mark the preliminary stages of your design, before making the final draft with indelible coloured markers.

If you are using trestles, G-clamps will help to secure your rug frame and prevent it from moving around. Masking tape can be used to protect hessian or tapestry canvas edges from fraying, as well as for sticking drawings and tracings onto the hessian when transferring your design.

Latex adhesive, rather than PVA, may be spread onto the back of a rug as a final process. This will prevent any fabrics from being dislodged, provide a non-slip surface – if the rug is to be placed on a hard floor – and make it easy to roll (rather than fold) if necessary. The same adhesive, generally available from hardware stores, is used for fixing carpet tiles. It is best to apply this with a card, plastic or metal spreader in a well-ventilated area.

Several tools and materials might be introduced for adding further decorative embellishment and interesting surfaces to your work, from a heat gun to felting equipment, and buttons, beads and discarded junk jewellery, which can be stuck or stitched into your work.

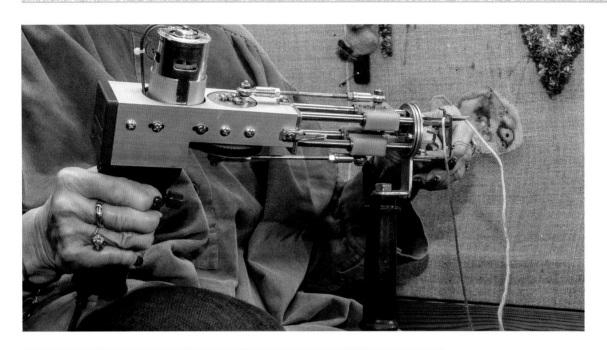

Above: The author threading one of her tufting guns with yarn.
© Lynne Stein

Left: The author working on the reverse side of the tufting cloth using recycled fabrics and yarns.
© Lynne Stein

Tufting guns

The technique of tufting is one that has gone viral, particularly since the start of the Covid pandemic, largely thanks to social media platforms such as TikTok and Instagram. No doubt witnessing the sped-up magic of achieving a sumptuous, colourful carpet creation with simply the pressing of a trigger has helped to create its mass appeal.

It involves the use of a specialised heavy-duty though lightweight tufting 'gun', which is used rather like a vertically operated handheld sewing machine, with a 'foot' that rests against the backing material, and its large protruding needle capable of penetrating fabric with tufts of yarn at considerable speed. Depending on the model, a knob at the base of the handle will adjust the speed. A domestic version of industrial tufting machines used for carpet-making, it is electrically operated, and thus a more costly and complex development from manual punch needle or rug hooking techniques.

Depending on the type of tufting gun, it will produce either a loop or cut pile on the other side of the backing cloth. The choice is very much dictated by both the appearance and textural feel required in the textile production. There are some more complicated tufting gun models that will do both by changing the settings, and even more sophisticated pneumatic models that require an air compressor. I use a combination of a heavier model with a wider needle for 'rags' and a lever for pile height adjustment, which I have used for many years, and a newer lighter model for yarns. Both produce a loop pile, much of which is left in that state, with any hand cutting and shearing being very much part of my creative process.

Additional equipment will include an appropriately sized frame, backing cloth, a threader, shears for cut-pile rugs, scissors, latex rug adhesive, a good range of yarns and in some cases 'rags'. Frames for stretching your backing cloth can be bought or constructed, and because of both the force of the tufting gun and the required tension of the backing cloth, should incorporate carpet gripper or carpet tack strips around the sides. Tufting backing cloth is strong, relatively lightweight, even-weave material, often with printed grid lines to aid your designs.

Many types and varieties of yarn can be used, including pure wool, cotton, silk, linen and synthetic fibres, as well as metallic and novelty yarns. These can be used both singly and in combination, and exciting effects – both visually and texturally – can be achieved with experimentation. If the yarn is on a cardboard cone, it will feed into the tufting gun more smoothly. It goes without saying that care should always be taken when operating this equipment.

Spider tools

Originally known as 'Catch It' tools, if used on a hessian backing cloth, spider tools provide a relatively easy, speedy and inexpensive way of creating a rag rug, while using up your stash of discarded clothing. There are two basic versions of the tool: one having a more pointed end than the other, which is easier for inserting through backing cloth. Creating a repetitive sturdy plaited or braided surface, it lends itself well to bold and less complex designs. Like rug hooking, if you are not completely satisfied with an area, it is simple enough to undo a particular part and rework it.

This technique can either be done with or without the use of a frame, although I prefer to use one. The spider tool can also be used simply as a braiding tool, rather like a crochet hook, using fabric strips, but without the need for a backing cloth.

Spider tool. © Lynne Stein

Depending on the nature and width of the fabric used, the effect achieved is similar to chain hooking. For more decorative purposes, the tool can also be used successfully with a variety of yarns, creating an embroidered chain stitch appearance. It can be combined successfully with other techniques described in this book, and with other types of backing cloth, such as loosely woven, knitted or crocheted surfaces.

Latch hooks

Particularly popular between the 1920s and 1960s and employed in many occupational therapy departments, the fairly simple technique of latch hooking can be used to create rugs, cushions and decorative wall art, and to embellish areas of textile. It is not suitable for making rag rugs, as no knots are required with this process and the tool does not easily accommodate strips of fabric. With the additional use of a colour chart or pre-printed pattern, it is capable of tackling images of considerable complexity as well as simpler, more graphic designs.

Like locker hooking, the use of a wide-mesh rug canvas as your foundation fabric dispenses with the need for a frame. The edges of your rug canvas can also be secured in a similar way to prevent fraying. For latch hooking, your canvas will normally have between three-and-a-half and five holes per inch, and if printed with a grid, this can be very helpful, particularly if your design is of a linear or geometric nature.

As well as a latch-hook tool, you will need a rug gauge, a variety of yarns and a marker. Smooth, non-slippery worsted or bulky weight woollen yarns work very well, but you may wish to experiment with different types, qualities and lengths. Pre-cut yarns tend to be 6.5 cm (2½ in) in length, but it is easy enough to create your own rug gauges (see circular seat pad, page 70) if you want to incorporate different pile heights in your work to emphasise sculptural and relief qualities. The latch-hook tool has either a straight or bent handle, neither being especially preferable, though you should find one with a comfortable handle to personally suit you.

Latch hook and assorted yarns. © Lynne Stein

Punch needles

Thanks to social media, the punch needle has only quite recently enjoyed a resurgence in popularity. However, its journey has a long history, dating back to the seventeenth century, having been used as an embellishment technique for clothing by Russian immigrants to the US. The tool has great potential for creating beautiful patterns and textures.

A range of tools and equipment for needle punching to suit projects of different sizes.
© Lynne Stein

There are several types, sizes, and makes of the tool. The size of the punch needle dictates the weight or thickness of yarn you use, as well as the height of the loop made. The Oxford punch needle is particularly satisfying to use. Whereas a threader for inserting the yarn is a necessary addition with most other punch needles, this make does not require one. Sizes range from 8 to 14. For bulkier yarns and even finely cut fabric strips, size 10 Regular is used to create taller loops. For finer yarns, such as certain knitting yarns and tapestry wool, the size 14 Mini will create shorter loops and is generally used for smaller scale and detail.

The Lavor punch needle with three needle sizes is also a good choice. It can be used with light worsted weight yarns and with cotton thread and embroidery floss for particularly fine work. The needle length and loop height can be adjusted by the screw on the side. Wool and acrylic blend yarns are generally satisfying for beginners to work with, giving an even surface and volume to the work. However, part of the craft's appeal is in experimenting with a range of colours, types, qualities and combinations of yarn, and observing the different results.

There are several sturdy even-weave fabrics for punching into; 100 per cent cotton monks cloth, which has twelve to fourteen holes per inch, is one of the most common choices. However, various types of linen, rug warp, and for certain projects even grey tufting cloth or hessian, can be used. Maintaining the tautness of the punching fabric, it can be stretched around a variety of frames depending on the scale, size and weight of the work being created. Stretcher bars, picture frames, gripper strip frames, plastic clip frames and circular embroidery hoops – particularly the invaluable No-Slip Morgan hoop – are all suitable.

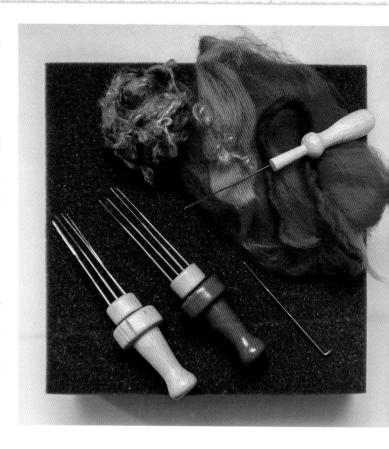

Needle-felting equipment.
© Lynne Stein

Needle-felting tools

Sculptural shapes and relief areas, as well as flat, painterly or graphic surfaces, can be achieved with this technique and successfully combined with other textile processes. You will need a felting pad or sponge, woollen fabric or pre-felt, Merino or certain other breeds of fleece tops or roving, and assorted woollen yarns. Fibres such as alpaca, angora and llama can also be successfully used. You should have several felting needles, as they tend to break easily. A needle holder is optional. For faster felting and larger areas, holders taking up to four needles are a possibility; however, for shapes within any of my projects, a single needle will suffice.

Different size or gauge needles produce different effects upon the wool. The higher the gauge, the more delicate the needle. Fine needles are suited to more decorative, detailed work, and the lower gauge needles are used for forming basic shapes; 36/38 gauge needles will suit most projects.

4 MAKING PROCESSES

Preparation

Cutting strips

It is sometimes difficult to establish precisely the amount of material needed for different areas of your design, and you may find it helpful to create a sample of that area first. The width of your fabric strip will depend upon its weight and quality, your chosen technique and the desired effect. For prodding, the average size of your pieces should be 7.5 × 2 cm (3 × ¾ in). The pieces can be cut in different ways, leaving straight, angled or pinked ends, which will affect the texture of your work.

A fabric gauge can be a useful tool, as it enables you to cut short, uniform strips, perfect for prodding. For hooking, you will need long strips, the width ranging from approximately 1 to 2.5 cm (⅓–1 in), depending on the fabric. For example, a soft nylon or polyester fabric would be cut into wider strips than thick, woollen sweater fabric. Generally, the thicker the fabric, the denser the appearance will be. A rotary cutter and mat can help in ensuring consistent strip widths. Certain garments, and fabrics like felt, can be folded first, allowing you to speed up the process by cutting through several layers simultaneously. Many fabrics, including cottons and organza, will tear well along the grain. A more frayed edge will be apparent, but combined with smoother non-fraying fabrics, interesting and attractive textural contrast can be achieved in your work. To obtain a long continuous length, make a small cut at the beginning of each length, repeating this process as you turn your fabric around to cut and tear it in the opposite direction. You will have angled corners on the fabric, but these can eventually be trimmed or will be hidden within your hooking.

Cutting pieces of fabric for prodding.

All photographs in this chapter © Lynne Stein

Stretching backing cloth

Most hooked work requires the use of some type of frame, depending on the size of your project. To aid ease of hooking and minimise physical strain, the backing cloth should be stretched as taut as possible when attaching it to the frame. To achieve straight and parallel edges, and for measurement accuracy, pull a thread from the hessian to give you a straight line.

If you are using a square mat-making frame or stretcher, place the frame over the centre of your backing cloth, ensuring the cloth's warp and weft are straight, to avoid eventual distortion of your design. You should then have a sufficient excess of cloth to fold around each side of the frame, which will also create further tension, once pinned or stapled. Start attaching the cloth along one side, at 5 cm (2 in) intervals, leaving the corners loose. Pulling the cloth taut, work the opposite side. Repeat this process on the remaining two sides, neatly folding in all excess backing cloth, and finally folding in the corners so that they have a mitred appearance.

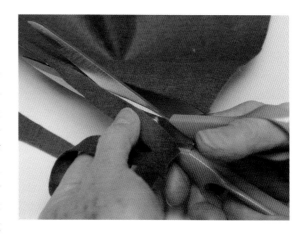

Cutting a continuous length of fabric for hooking.

If you are using a large adjustable rug frame, the hemmed design on your backing cloth should be placed centrally and stitched with strong linen thread to the lengths of webbing on each long side of your frame. The width of your work will be determined by the length of your webbing, but since the backing is rolled around the rug frame as the work progresses, its length is limitless.

Transferring designs

When transferring your design, bear in mind that if it is going to be worked in the prodded method, it should be drafted onto the reverse side of your backing cloth, which, since done from back to front, will be facing you as you proceed. Otherwise, in most cases, the design would be drafted directly onto the right side of the cloth. Whether the design is drafted before or after stretching the cloth, take care not to distort the design.

Stretching and attaching the backing cloth to the frame with a staple gun, showing a mitred corner.

If freehand drawing does not come easily to you, there are several options for transferring an entire design onto your backing cloth. The use of a photocopier or a scanner and printer for the purposes of enlarging or reducing a design can be invaluable. It might be necessary to repeat this process several times, turning the image to fit, to achieve the required size.

You can create stiff card templates of the overall and basic shapes in your design. Draw around these, first with tailor's chalk, and then with an indelible marker, which should be broad tipped, to cope with the coarseness of hessian.

A transfer pencil or tracing wheel, tracing paper and an iron can be used. Having traced your design with the transfer pencil, pin the drawn side of the paper facing the backing cloth and press with a hot, dry iron. To avoid overheating either surface, rather than gliding the iron, move it systematically across the design, with vertical movements, ensuring all areas are subjected to heat. Bear in mind that the transferred design will be the reverse of the original.

Alternatively, a darning needle can be used to prick holes along the design's outlines. Once the punctured tracing paper is positioned on the backing cloth, pounce or powdered tailor's chalk should be sprinkled over the drawn area, its penetration through the holes being aided by a soft-bristle toothbrush. The outlines can then be redefined with an indelible marker. Similarly, if the design is drawn onto tissue paper and pinned to the backing cloth, small running stitches should be sewn along the outlines of the design. The tissue paper can then be carefully separated from the stitched backing cloth, and the outlines clarified with a marker pen.

Your original design can be overlaid with an acetate sheet grid, the equal grid squares becoming a guide for making it larger or smaller. The more detailed your design, the smaller the grid squares should be. The same even grid should be drawn on your backing cloth, with the scale adjusted as required. Working square by square, copy the markings from the original grid to the backing cloth, until the designs match. You could use tailor's chalk initially, and then an indelible marker once you are satisfied with the result.

Dressmaker's or artist's carbon paper is useful too. Placing the ink side facing the cloth, pin your design over the carbon paper and draw firmly over the outlines with a dressmaker's pencil until the markings are sufficiently transferred.

A lightbox can be improvised by taping your heavily outlined design on thin paper to a clear glass window and placing the fabric over the design. The natural light should reveal the design clearly, enabling it to be traced.

Card templates, grid marked hessian and corresponding acetate grid overlay on the rug design.

Strong, sheer fabric such as tulle can be used as a transfer fabric. Once bearing the traced design, this should be positioned securely on your backing cloth, the outlines being traced with an indelible marker, ensuring that they seep through to the cloth.

Techniques

The techniques described below can be used separately or can be combined in a project to produce an increased range of textured surfaces. The type of project will usually dictate the technique and the fabrics you select. For example, if you want to create a soft, warm rug of subtle-toned, abstract design, you might choose to work this entirely by prodding, using dyed, recycled woollen fabrics. By contrast, a decorative wall hanging might include several techniques and methods of embellishment with a broad palette and range of fabrics and fibres.

Hooking

It is important to be comfortable when hooking, and positioning your frame at an angle to suit you is crucial. Remember to reposition your work as it progresses if using a large rug frame; also remember that you have the option of working from either side, rather than over-stretching and hurting your back. Getting up from your work every half hour or so and having a good stretch is vital.

Working with the right side of the design facing you, the hook should be held like a pencil with the hand you would normally use. If right-handed, you will find it easier to work from right to left, and vice versa if you are left-handed. Poking downwards through the backing cloth to create a space in the weave, your hook, facing the direction of hooking, should be ready to catch your fabric strip underneath, which is held between the thumb and forefinger of your other hand. This position of the hand will constantly feed the fabric onto the base of the hook. The end of the strip should be pulled through to start the row of loops, leaving a first tuft of approximately 1 cm (½ in) on the top surface.

Continue this motion, next pulling a slightly shorter loop up above the surface of the backing cloth. As you continue forming a row of loops, try to create a reasonably even pile height, and an even space between the loops themselves, with just one or two warp threads of the backing cloth between, depending on the weight and thickness of your fabric. Creating a dense surface pile will prevent the work from dislodging; aesthetically, you will usually want to hide any visible backing cloth with the loops of your design. When finishing a fabric strip, bring the end to the top surface, trimming the beginning

Hooking a row of loops along the outline.

and end of your hooking to the height of the loops. The reverse of your work should simply show a flat connected running stitch row.

Your loops should be hooked systematically in rows to prevent unworked areas of the design from being blocked and creating bulkiness on the reverse. However, these rows can be vertical, horizontal, diagonal or swirly, rhythmic lines, the direction of your hooking affecting its textural appearance. This technique is particularly suited to detailed, figurative and pictorial areas, and for creating subtle colour and textural blends. Certain designs may also call for longer or irregular loops in areas of your hooking. You can also experiment with pile height, and with blending different fabrics and yarns.

Prodding

This technique can be done on your lap, without the use of a frame. With the reverse side of the backing cloth facing you, use your prodder to make a hole or space, and push half of your short piece of fabric through the hole, leaving one end underneath and the other on top. With an average space of a few warp threads, push the other end through to the right side, so that a tuft of two ends of fabric will have formed on the right side, and a flat stitch on the reverse. Repeat this process, pushing one end of the next piece of fabric into or close by the space holding the last piece. Your spacing will depend on the thickness and weight of the fabric, and on the desired density of pile. It will take time before the design on the right side becomes apparent, as the technique relies upon the completion of juxtaposed areas to clarify each other's shapes. The tufts can finally be adjusted on the right side, and although this is a basic and simple technique, they can be trimmed, sculpted, stitched, painted and embellished, to create rich surfaces.

Alternatively, this sort of surface can be worked with a spring-clip tool, sometimes known as a rag-rugger or bodger. In this case, the work is done from the front, pulling each fabric strip through two or three threads in your hessian with the tweezer-like action of the tool. The number of strips pulled through will dictate the density of pile, and you should try to ensure that they

Prodding.

The prodded surface.

are worked closely enough to prevent any exposure of the hessian, or any of the pieces falling out. An average spacing of four or five hessian threads usually works well.

Chain hooking

The effect achieved is similar in appearance to embroidered chain stitch, but is thicker and more substantial. It is also similar to the surface created with the spider tool. You will need a hook and a similar length of rag strip as for hooking. Poke the hook through the backing cloth, and bring the first fabric strip end to the top surface. Insert the hook again, a small distance away, this time pulling a loop through. With the first loop remaining on the hook, and using the same consistent spacing between loops, poke the hook through again, drawing up a second loop. Create the first link by slipping the first loop over the second, gently pulling the stitch flat across the backing cloth's surface. Repeat this motion, forming a chained line. It is worth experimenting with different thicknesses, weights and textures of fabric.

Chain hooking.

Fleece and yarn sculpting

With effects comparable to the Waldoboro technique (see page 22), this is done in exactly the same way as hooking, but instead of rag strips, teased-out strips of fleece tops or roving are used. Alternatively, you can use several strands of yarn simultaneously, such as carpet wool, mohair or alpaca, or a combination of fleece and yarn. Your loops should be at least 2.5 cm (1 in) in height and packed extremely closely together. To thicken the pile, you can hook further loops within the work, carefully avoiding creating bulkiness on the reverse. Once the area is sufficiently dense, cut and carve your desired shape with a very sharp pair of scissors. This technique can add a delicious tactile quality to your work and is useful for creating shapes and areas such as furrowed fields, facial features, motifs and circular shapes.

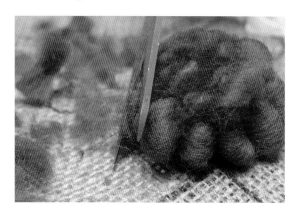

Cutting and sculpting the hooked fleece loops.

Wire wrapping

Wrapping wire with yarn is ideal for creating fluid lines to outline and embellish areas, or to include lettering in your work. Flexible millinery wire, electrical wire and plastic scoobies are ideal as the core for wrapping. It is advisable to have hooked your preliminary area, on which the wrapping will be attached, first, unless the wrapping itself will form an extra appendage.

Establish the approximate length of wire you will need for the shape and use a liberal length of yarn to wrap. To avoid leaving any unsightly knots on the reverse of your work, thread your wire or scoobie onto a wide-eyed needle and insert it through the top surface of the work, leaving half the total length of wire there. From underneath, in the next space, bring the needle and remaining wire back up to the top surface, so that you have an anchored double strand of wire on the top to work with.

Wrapping a scoobie with woollen yarn.

With your chosen thread either single or doubled, start by attaching the yarn to the wire with several lark's head knots (see Step 6 of the birdie tote bag project on page 123 for how to do this), and gently push these down to the base of the wire, tightening them. Holding the wire core taut, you can either repeat this process so that the wrapped strand is edged, or for a smooth, tubular appearance, start wrapping the thread around the wire. Periodically push downwards, smoothing it, after wrapping at approximately 1 cm (½ in) intervals, until you have achieved the desired length. Position it into your required shape, then couch it in place, using a length of the same wrapping yarn. Stitch at 5 mm (¼ in) intervals over both the wrapped wire and the worked surface underneath. You can vary the width and texture of your wrapping by using different cores and yarns.

Braiding.

Braiding

Braiding can be used as a technique for making rugs on its own, either by coiling or stitching together strips, or you can use it to create borders for other types of rug.

Taking three strips of fabric approximately 5 cm (2 in) wide, secure the ends with a large safety pin, hooking this over a static object such as a cup hook or coat peg. Roll up each strip of fabric, fastening each end with a pin and gradually release the rolls as you work to avoid them becoming tangled. Begin braiding or plaiting close to the pin, bringing the right strip across the middle one, and then the left strip over the new middle one, trying to achieve a consistent tension and a smooth, flat braid. Try to conceal any raw edges by turning them under towards the reverse or inner side of the braid as you progress. Continue until you have enough strips for your project, pinning at the end of each braid length to secure. Remove the pin from the start of the braid, stitch it to conceal any raw edges and taper this end.

Working on a flat surface, coil the braids, which have already been stitched end to end, sewing through the sides of each braid to connect them for a circular rug. Alternatively, place them alongside one another and stitch through one side of a braid to the next with a long or curved needle until all strips are sewn together and a rectangle is formed. To create a border, check that your braid is long enough, and carefully wrap and stitch it around the rug's outer edge. Experiment with different combinations of tones and colourways, as well as fabrics.

Using a spider tool

I find it considerably easier to use the more pointed version of this tool (see oval rag runner, page 105) and to stretch the backing cloth onto a suitable sturdy frame, once the outline shape and any details have been drawn onto it. A large rug frame is not essential, as it is simple enough to detach the work and move it around the frame as the work progresses.

Several types of material can be incorporated, particularly smooth, stretchy fabrics such as T-shirts and leggings. It is important that the fabric strips will thread through the tool's holes smoothly. A width of between 1.2 cm (½ in) and 2 cm (¾ in) should be prepared, dependent upon the weight and thickness of the fabric.

The fabric strip should be threaded through both holes of the tool along the concave side, starting at the hole near the handle, leaving a small length of the strip protruding beyond the top hole and most of the strip trailing by the handle. With your tool underneath the hessian, wiggle its tip through to the front surface and push it through a loop in the fabric strip, while gently pushing the index finger of your other hand through the loop.

Draw the spider tool back downwards and out of the hessian. Leaving a small

Threading the spider tool with a strip of fabric.

space, reinsert it, repeating the first step and allowing the loop in the fabric strip to be placed around the tool. Use your spare hand and always keep the fabric strip relatively loose. Once the spider tool is pushed right through to the front surface, the first link of your chain will be apparent. Continue this process, pushing each new loop through the previous one so that a firm, secure row of chain links is created.

Once a strip of fabric has been finished, the end should be left underneath and a new strip begun in the same way, inserting it first into the same space as the end of the last strip. This will leave two ends of fabric next to each other, which can be trimmed neatly when finishing the work.

An overlap of approximately 5 cm (2 in) should be left for turning under and hemming the work.

Working carefully from the front surface so that no chain links are disturbed, or excess hessian is showing, this can be stitched in place. The reverse surface can then be spread with latex and lined with a suitable fabric.

Locker hooking

Using a wide-mesh rug canvas, three to five holes per inch, makes a frame unnecessary for this technique because of the canvas's stiffness. Size 5 rug canvas will allow for rather more detail. Hessian can be used as a backing cloth in some cases, for a more free-flowing design. Dependent upon the desired effect, your long fabric strips should be approximately 1.5–2.5 cm (½–1 in) wide. The edges of your design can be secured either temporarily with masking tape or by mitring the hemmed corners, and using a rug needle and yarn, oversewing these and the folded canvas surplus beyond your design.

Using a 180 cm (6 ft) length of colour co-ordinated yarn or cotton twine for the locking medium, thread one end through the eye of your locker hook and tie the other to the starting square of the canvas. Hold the strip of fabric horizontally underneath the canvas, leaving a 5 cm (2 in) excess. Poke the hook end of the needle through the hole and pull a 5 mm (¼ in) height loop of material through to the top surface of the rug canvas. Keep the loop on your hook and go into the next hole, repeating this process until you have created a row of up to ten loops. Gently pull your threaded locker hook through all the loops, releasing them and ensuring that the locker medium is taut and holds them in place. Continue this process with a new row of loops and the same length of yarn, introducing new material strips and different colours and fabrics as necessary.

Unlike hooking, the ends of the yarn or locking medium should be left on the top surface, whereas the fabric ends should be left underneath to be threaded through loops and trimmed at the end. Combining vertical and horizontal rows, the direction of your hooking will influence the ultimate appearance of your work.

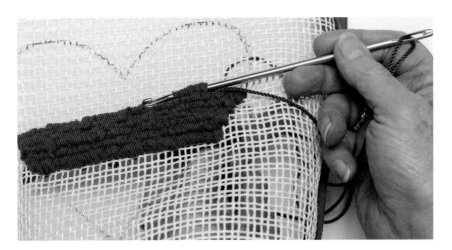

Locker hooking.

Latch hooking

Start your work at the lower left-hand side of the canvas if you're right-handed (and the opposite side if you're left-handed). Fold the length of your yarn and loop it around the base of the latch hook, between the handle and the latch. Push the hook and latch through the space in one square underneath a stiff line of your canvas, so that they both pass underneath it. Drawing it back through the square in front to the top surface of the canvas, position the loop ends over the canvas line, between the latch and the hook. Close the latch and pull your hook handle back firmly, so that a secure slip knot is formed and the yarn ends appear on the top surface of the canvas. Continue this process, working systematically in rows as your design and colours dictate, progressing across and working from the bottom to the top of your canvas.

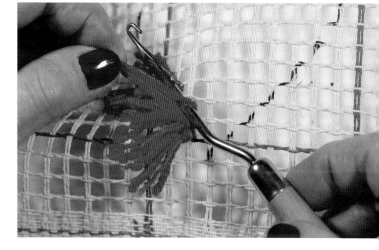

Top: Latch-hook sampling with a variety of yarns, fabrics, fibres and plastic.

Above: Latch hooking pre-cut yarn through rug canvas.

Needle punching

As you will discover, the craft is easy to learn and progresses quickly. It is a versatile medium for creating both functional and decorative items of different scales and sizes. Like so many of the techniques included in this book, it is also very addictive!

Left: Needle punching a design which has been stretched onto a gripper rod frame with protective covers along the sides.

Below: Needle punch sampling on monks cloth on a plastic clip frame.

Once you have threaded your needle and stretched the punching cloth on your hoop or frame, hold your work free from any work surface underneath, including your legs! Dependent upon your punch needle and yarn choice, there should only be approximately 3 mm (⅛ in) between punches. Without any knots involved, if the correct foundation material and yarn are used and both are kept taut as you punch, this will ensure that continuous and consistent loops of yarn are held in place in your cloth. Penetrating your fabric until the handle of the punch needle touches the cloth, the needle is then drawn out again, the tip barely resurfacing between each 'stitch'. The punching is done on one side of the cloth, which will ultimately become either the reverse or front surface of the work. The punched side will have a series of flat connected stitches, comparable to embroidery. The other side will have a relief looped pile with a fine carpet-like appearance.

Simple, bold graphic designs are best suited to the craft, but by adjusting and/or trimming loop heights and combining yarn tones and textures, exciting effects can be achieved. The results can have a similar appearance to rug hooking but notably require a different action and reverse process, and are predominantly yarn-based. Dependent upon the nature of your project, you may want to seal and protect it by spreading a fine layer of latex or textile adhesive across the reverse side.

Needle felting

Because felting needles are barbed, their repetitive 'stabbing' causes the fibres to interlock with one another, creating a more compact woollen fabric. Always work with a sponge or brush mat underneath the work, to support it and absorb the impact of the needle.

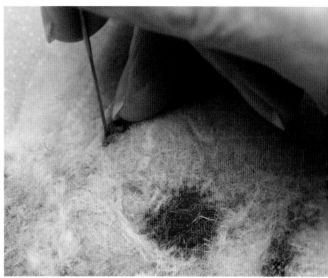

Felting needles are extremely sharp, and so care should be taken not to prick yourself while working! They are also quite delicate, and to avoid breakage you should try to hold the felting needle, stabbing it in a straight up-and-down motion through the layers of fibres, working on a small area at a time until the layers start to mesh. The more you work into an area, the more pronounced your indentations will become. The fibres from the top surface will be partially poked through to the reverse of the cloth. Keep turning the fabric, to prevent it from adhering to the sponge or pad. Work each side until you have achieved the desired effect with tones and textures. You may even find that the reverse side becomes the more interesting surface for continuing your felting.

Needle felting.

To build up a relief area, either use extra fleece or create several cut shapes of fabric or pre-felt, each slightly decreasing in size, and layer these upon your base surface before positioning your fleece and fibres over them and starting to needle felt. A foam core or an armature of pipe cleaners can be used for constructing the base of a three-dimensional form.

Sampling

It is possible to create interesting marks, textures and surfaces within your work by using and combining different techniques, fabrics and yarns. I like to emphasise the sheer value of 'playing' and experimentation. You need only be restricted by the limits of your imagination!

Basic hooking and prodding, as well as several other techniques included in this book, can be combined with knitting, stitch and other textile processes, such as appliqué, chain hooking and stitching, French or spool knitting, felting and crochet, to achieve rich and tactile surfaces. Creating experimental sample areas can often inform and inspire a larger-scale piece of work, and this process can certainly be useful to try out preliminary ideas.

Be prepared to try less conventional materials, and combinations of techniques and processes, exploring different colour schemes, scales and textural possibilities within your work. It is useful to observe and note how different fabrics and fibres behave, individually and when combined with others. For instance, the loops of an area of hooked felt fabric will be more solid, sturdy

Far left: Fleece sculpting and wire wrapping encased by prodded hand-painted silk.

Left: A wide variety of fabrics and fibres, including net, foil-printed Lycra, pierced rubber and rickrack braid, combined with beading and wire wrapping.

and vertical than those done with nylon or polyester. Certain patterned fabrics, because of the twist that occurs from time to time when hooking or using the spider tool, will occasionally expose the paler printed version on their reverse side, creating an overall tonal appearance. As well as patterned fabrics, batiked and silk-painted swatches, and space-dyed yarns can generate unusual marks and colourings in your work. Frayed edges of furnishing linens and novelty yarns produce interesting irregular surfaces. Using pinking shears to trim the ends of a prodded area or to cut the entire pieces of fabric will produce a serrated textural surface. Hooked, prodded, braided, stitched or punched, you could try incorporating unusual materials such as plastic packaging, balloons, foam

Far left: Hooked silk fabrics and raised wrapped wire loops of textured and space-dyed yarn.

Above: Stitched decorative braids echoing the printed silver Lycra.

rubber, raffia and straw, fur, outdated bank notes, gauzy satsuma packaging, metallic and space-dyed yarns, and even human hair into your work. Once again, part of the fun with this medium will be the rummaging and collecting.

Embellishment

Scribbled net

White or cream polyester, nylon net and certain synthetic lace fabrics work best with this process. Use fabric crayons and markers applied directly onto the fabric. Make random marks with your colours, leaving enough of the fabric blank to contrast. Fix the 'scribbled' design by applying a hot iron to the reverse of the fabric, according to manufacturer's instructions. Cut pieces for prodding from your fabric with scissors. Because of the nature of the fabric and the unpredictability of the marks, you will find that you can achieve a lovely ethereal quality with scribbled net.

Heat bonding

All sorts of leftover papers, threads, tiny fabric offcuts, sequins and small beads can be used here. To enable these to bond, an assortment of plastic-based materials, such as bubble wrap, laminating pouches, plastic bath scrubs and other waste material can be used. On top of a thick towel and a sheet of non-stick baking parchment, create a layered 'sandwich' of these materials, strategically arranging colours and shapes. Make the work slightly bigger than the shape that you ultimately want. Place over this another sheet of non-stick baking parchment, and iron on top with a hot iron. Once it has sufficiently melted and slightly cooled, peel the baking parchment away from the plastic and trim the shape to size. These can be used between areas of hooking or other textile surface, attaching with an all-purpose adhesive, or by making holes with a thick needle and applying them like buttons. Heat bonding should always be done in a well-ventilated area, wearing a protective mask to protect against any toxic fumes.

Scribbled net.

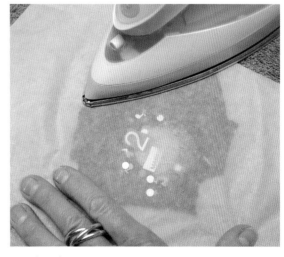

Heat bonding.

Shisha mirrors

Although bought shisha mirrors are available in different sizes, you can also achieve the look by saving tiny mirror offcuts, or applying tin foil to

Securing the outlined shisha mirror.

card circles and completing the effect of both these options with an outer plastic or metal ring, bound with beautiful threads or narrow strips of fabric such as silk. The ring should be wrapped similarly to the wire-wrapping technique. The excess thread should be used to neatly stitch or couch the embellishment in place, on top of or within the hooked or textile surface.

Pom-poms

These can be bought in various sizes and colours. However, for edging or embellishing a rug or wall hanging, you can make your own in a variety of ways. They can be wet-felted, using hot soapy water and moulded in your hands. For needle-felted pom-poms, I use carpet wool thrums for the core: create a spherical shape by winding the wool around your finger until you have the desired size. Place fleece around the sphere and using a felting needle (see page 49) to lock the fibres, create a smooth, solid ball. This can be left plain or decorated with stitch, beads, or sequins, or with needle-felted detail.

Alternatively, you can use strips of pure woollen woven or knitted fabric, such as a mohair scarf or blanket. The strip width should be in accordance with the chosen size of your pom-pom. Once you have made the required number of spheres, insert them, one at a time, into an old pair of tights, separating them with tightly knotted yarn. Set them on the hottest wash cycle of your machine, together with another coarse item, such as a towel, for friction. Pom-poms can also be made in the traditional way, so favoured in primary-school projects.

Junk jewellery, shells, glass, pebble or slate slices, and dyed, sanded coconut shell, are among the many items that might be used to embellish and enhance a piece of non-functional work. They can be glued or stitched into the textile in a variety of ways.

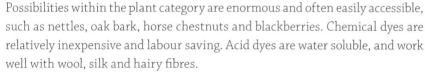

Left: Different sizes of felted balls made using a variety of methods and fibres.

Below: Needle felting a spherical shape.

Dyeing

Although for me part of the pleasure in making rag rugs is in the sourcing and collecting of a diversity of fabrics, experimenting with dyeing and overdyeing fabrics can be fun, and can produce a range of interesting and closely related tones and hues which might otherwise not be easy to find.

Natural and synthetic dyes are derived from animals, plants and minerals, for example cochineal, kermes, indigo, onion skins, iron buff and ochre. Possibilities within the plant category are enormous and often easily accessible, such as nettles, oak bark, horse chestnuts and blackberries. Chemical dyes are relatively inexpensive and labour saving. Acid dyes are water soluble, and work well with wool, silk and hairy fibres.

All colours can be mixed from the basic primary colours – red, yellow and blue – with or without the addition of black. Adding more of the dye's complementary colour to a dye bath will darken or tone down the eventual colour. Similarly, many fabrics can be overdyed in a weak or light dye bath to mute or transform their existing colours. To achieve an uneven, mottled effect, the space for the amount of fabric within the dye bath should be cramped.

The existing colour of a fabric can be removed by immersing it in a simmering solution of ammonia for a few minutes. Fabric can be simmered for approximately half an hour, in a solution of either salt or vinegar, in order to set a new colour, making it dye-fast. Salt opens the pores of the fabric, increasing its ability to absorb the dye, and also dulls colour, whereas vinegar will brighten and enhance it. It should finally be rinsed well. This process has better results with predominantly natural fibres. There are also commercial dye removers, if the colour is hard to extract.

Direct dyes, for all natural fabrics including wool, cotton, silk, straw and linen, can be ideal for rag rugs and wall hangings. Disperse dyes, including the stove-top variety, are suited to synthetic fabrics and fibres. Fibre-reactive Procion dyes which, like acid dyes, are normally supplied in the form of granules or powder, include both hot- and cold-water methods. The processes, done either by hand or in a washing machine, are suitable for natural fibres, and have the highest rate of adherence. Cold-water dyes have the advantage of being usable outdoors. The intensity of the range of colours can easily be adjusted by the strength of the dyebath. Tie-dye and batik effects can be achieved with cold-water dyeing, and can sometimes be done in a microwave, where a mottled or uneven appearance can be obtained, if desired. Some multi-purpose dyes may be suitable for certain materials, including leather, Lycra, raffia and plastics.

If the dyeing process as a preliminary task appeals, it can be both fascinating and helpful to keep a record of your dyeing experiments. Note the type of dye, fabric or fibre type, dyeing time, any pre-treatments and number of immersions, accompanied by a small swatch of the achieved colour. Also, if you know that certain household or clothing items are not dye-fast and will bleed their colours when washed, you might wish to experimentally place some fabrics together with these in a machine wash, finally fixing them with your chosen method. This can often result in a range of paler, subtle tones, both on plain and patterned fabrics. Just as kippers were once used to extract fabric dyes for rag rugs, it is perfectly possible, with the addition of salt, to make a dyebath from the contents of your fruit bowl, vegetable rack or kitchen cupboards, such as saffron, turmeric, red cabbage, beetroot, spinach, kale, certain fruit skins, coffee and tea.

Other useful equipment might include an enamel pot, to be used solely for dyeing, measuring spoons and cups, rods and dowels, a heatproof measuring jug, wide-necked plastic-lidded storage jars, labels, rubber gloves and a notebook. It is advisable to wear old clothes and an apron, and depending upon the dye, a facemask. Work in a well-ventilated area. For disposal, dye solutions should be diluted and poured down an outside drain.

Finishing

How you finish your project will depend largely upon its size, its function and the process, fabrics and fibres used to create it.

Finishing a hooked or prodded rug

It has always been debatable whether a rag rug should be backed. Backing a rug with hessian can be problematic, since dirt and grit can settle between the two layers, adversely affecting the right side. However, coating the back of the rug first with latex adhesive will help to prevent this, and will also prevent any loops or tufts from disappearing. As appropriate, hessian, felt or heavy cotton can be used for backing. For smaller items, such as pictures, pillows or jewellery, a softer material can be used.

When backing a rug, carpet-binding tape can be used but, as it shrinks considerably, should always be washed first. It can be dyed to match the colour of your work. Take your rug off the frame, if used, trimming around the edges so that there is a backing cloth excess of 5–7.5 cm (2–3 in). Turn this under all the way round, bonding it to the reverse with latex. Having cut and hemmed the edges of a slightly smaller piece of backing cloth, position this on top of the reverse, attaching the two surfaces with latex. If necessary, complete the process by gluing carpet binding all the way round the reverse of the rug, mitring the corners.

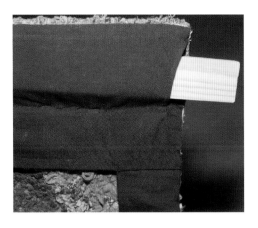

Batten slotted through an extra sleeve in the lining of the wall hanging.

Finishing a wall hanging

If you are attaching a wall hanging to a mounting board and framing, no backing is necessary. To finish a smaller pictorial piece, turn in the backing cloth approximately 2.5 cm (1 in) beyond the outer edge of the design, all the way round the work. With small stitches, sew carefully from the right side, between any loops or tufts. Spread latex adhesive thinly across the reverse and allow to dry.

Back a wall hanging with a sufficiently heavy and durable fabric, allowing enough for a hem. Avoid making this too taut as this will prevent the piece from hanging properly. Placing the backing on the reverse, pin along each turned-under edge, mitring the corners. Stitch the edges neatly with strong thread.

Another hanging method is to stitch strong tape loops or create a further long fabric sleeve along the top of the reverse, through which a batten or pole can be slotted. Heavy-duty Velcro, stitched to both ends of the textile's reverse and attached to battens which are fixed to the wall, is another successful option.

Cleaning and care

Surface dust and grime can be carefully removed with a low-suction vacuum cleaner attachment. If the work is very delicate and incorporates an assortment of fabrics and fibres, a sheet or nylon monofilament screen can be placed over an area as you clean. However, if the fabrics are more durable, and the reverse has been coated with latex, protecting the weaker hessian threads, the work can be gently shaken or beaten outside. Any spills or staining should be tackled immediately with a towel or absorbent kitchen paper, sponging with lukewarm water, taking care not to over-moisten the fibres. A weak solution of white vinegar or household ammonia should remove any difficult stains. When not in use, your rugs should be rolled with the top surface facing outwards and stored in a dry environment, within layers of bubble wrap, and an outer cotton bag.

5 RECYCLE, UPCYCLE...

I would be the first to admit that I can get some very strange looks as I scrutinise skips, gape longingly at litter and wander apparently aimlessly through supermarket aisles, scanning the shelves not so much for delectable edibles as for the most interesting beer bottle tops and colourful printed foil biscuit wrappers!

The notion of turning trash into treasure is a magical one which exists at the very heart of creativity. With open eyes and mind, new, stylish and often witty uses can be found and fashioned from reclaimed, everyday and often unremarkable objects. The idea of these having had a previous life, with a story to tell, often provides the necessary spark and stimulus for a new creation.

Rejected and unwanted items, given a different context, can very often have a fresh aesthetic appeal, revealing attractive qualities with essentially human connections. The surface of a recycled pre-loved object may be worn and withered, rusted or corroded, its painted or printed image perhaps blurred or faded, inviting subtle transformation or an entirely new identity by the addition of different materials and processes.

Recycling and upcycling are activities associated with thrift. There is a certain freedom in making, afforded by the fact that obtaining these articles often comes at little or no financial cost, allowing playful experimentation and mistakes to be made. It is often, in my experience, those mistakes that end up being the most fruitful!

In tune with the times, this area of recycling is also eco-friendly and beneficial for the environment, creatively addressing issues connected with sustainable living and waste management, even if in a relatively small way.

Undoubtedly, a vital aspect of rag-rug making – whether by hand, with a tufting gun or with the spider tool – will involve sourcing and using a rich diversity of recycled fabrics. Browsing in charity and thrift shops will occasionally introduce you to items of clothing which, at first sight, in their original state, may seem ugly and outdated. However, the inclusion of such fabrics often provides unexpected richness. A worn and unattractive jacket may have wonderful vintage Bakelite buttons; a belt buckle on a coat or jacket may be just the shape you were looking for. Interesting embroidered or printed patches or labels might provide inspiration. Knitwear can be felted in a hot machine wash,

Left: *Café do Brasil*. Ben Hall. Hooked without a frame. Coloured denim, cotton, leather, tea-dyed wool blanket strips.
© Ben Hall

Below: *Postcard from Helsinki*. Kaisa Takala, Minna Piironen, Hanna-Liisa Pykala, 2010. Plastic packaging waste knotted around building construction mesh. © Kaisa Takala, Minna Piironen, Hanna-Liisa Pykala

later being cut into strips, stitched upon, or simply unravelled to reuse the yarn. But this is far from the end of the story! I hope that many of the examples and projects shown in this book will fire your imagination and help you to consider the vast range of commonplace objects that, instead of being discarded, could be incorporated within your work in the most personal and exciting ways.

Even rag-rug tools and backing cloths, as history has already indicated, can be fashioned from existing objects. I have found that a lacquered chopstick can be a fine tool for prodding, and a

large paperclip can be stretched out and reshaped to become an efficient threader for a wide aperture punch needle or your tufting gun. A vegetable sack, as well as providing suitable backing cloth, might inspire a piece of work because of its attractive central printed design. Plastic building and garden meshes can also have their uses, particularly for an exterior project, which might involve using recycled packaging for the 'weft' materials.

When thinking about decorative patterns and borders, the flotsam and jetsam seen during a walk on the beach, as well as interesting pieces of beached glass, shells, pebbles, feathers, driftwood and stones, can both inform and contribute to a piece of work, whichever tools and techniques you decide to use. Ring pulls

Left: Charity shop knitwear embellished with rows of latch-hooked yarns, 2021. © Lynne Stein

Below: Needle-punched and beaded fish encased in a washed-out sardine tin, 2021. © Lynne Stein

from tin cans, sliced corks, and inverted or hammered bottle tops can all be useful additions. Sanded pieces of dried coconut shell, painted with acrylics or dyed with wood stains, drilled and stitched, or attached to your backing cloth with adhesive, create a rich surface when encased within fabrics and beadwork. Junk jewellery, buttons and beads, eco-friendly PET plastic sequins and also glass nuggets used for floristry provide decorative interest and texture; curtain rings can be wrapped with thread or fabric, covering pieces of mirror, or foil-covered card, to mimic shisha mirrors.

Sample. Hooked biscuit wrappers, sanded and dyed coconut shell, beading and stitched rickrack braid, 2012.
© Lynne Stein

Parts of toys, such as a small car wheel, a doll's head or even a painted zoo or farmyard animal, might all prove to be exciting finds. Household articles and items of clothing that have seen better days, such as old faded tea towels, a crocheted doily, metal pan scourers and plastic bath scrubs, might all find their way into your work. A knitted or crocheted beanie hat or jumper might provide a suitable surface upon which to add flamboyant latch-hooked areas of embellishment. Trays, picture frames and painting canvases might be suitable for mounting or framing a pictorial piece. Metal and plastic bottle and carton tops, and even sardine tins could be salvaged for containing and displaying badges, buttons and other small-scale pieces of work.

As you saw in the Embellishment section (on pages 51–2), many materials, objects and artefacts can be reworked and transformed. Metals can be drilled, hammered, punctured, painted or rusted. Some polymer-based materials, once heat is applied, will shrink, blister and laminate, and experimentation can lead to the creation of interesting buttons, beads and other forms. However, it is important that appropriate measures are taken to ensure your safety when doing so, such as wearing a mask and working in a well-ventilated area.

Not least of all, fruit punnets and containers and small glass herb pots can provide useful storage solutions for your buttons, beads, junk jewellery and other embellishment items.

The creative potential involving reclaimed, recycled and upcycled materials is infinite. As well as involving less expense, the satisfaction derived from fashioning something unique, while addressing environmental concerns and giving new meaning to 'clutter', is always worthwhile.

6 THE CREATIVE EYE: Sources of Inspiration

Any number of available articles and objects can provide starting points for your work. These might include printed material such as greeting cards and wrapping papers, patterns on clothing and furnishing fabrics, jewellery design and ceramic decoration, or a section of a painting, whether detailed and figurative or alternatively bold and abstract.

Selecting the appropriate technique for a specific project is vital to the ultimate appearance of your work, and since the various tools and techniques are capable of achieving quite different surfaces and textures, such decisions might be important at the early stages of your design process. For example, if a blurred and rather Impressionistic appearance is desired, the prodded or latch-hooked technique would be more suitable. If great definition and detail are required, hooking or needle punch are more appropriate choices. However, as shown throughout this book, a range of techniques can be introduced and combined with each other to suit a project, the choices being influenced both functionally and aesthetically.

Narratives in the form of song lyrics, legends, nursery rhymes, poems or stories might inspire you, just as a piece of family memorabilia might spark off the core of an idea.

Visiting galleries and museums will offer endless opportunities for browsing through collections and discovering works of aesthetic appeal and personal relevance. Different seasons will allow you to focus on the shifting shapes and tones of landscape and nature. Rows of vegetables growing in an urban allotment might provide the focus for stylised rhythmic and repetitive patterns; and summer gardens in full bloom can serve as a necessary reminder and living proof of the magic of colour.

Many of the people who have attended my workshops over the years have been keen to depict their domestic pets – a marmalade cat, or on one memorable occasion, a pot-bellied pig! A trip to the zoo or an aquarium can be a wonderful way of

Pathway Well Worn (detail), Lynne Stein, 2008. 132 × 84 cm (52 × 33 in). Handhooked, needle felting, stitch. Largely recycled mixed fabrics and fibres, plastics, rubber and paper.

All images in this chapter © Lynne Stein

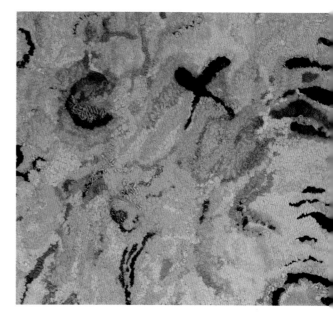

La Mer (detail). Lynne Stein, 1990. 128 × 126 cm (50½ × 49½ in). Gun-tufted. Largely recycled fabrics and fibres on polyester backing cloth. Always working from the reverse of the backing cloth, the tufting gun enables both relief convex shapes and compact, mosaic-like surfaces to be created.

engaging children in drawing activities, which can in turn inspire your own work. As I frequently emphasise, children's art can be perfectly suited to all techniques, and drawings from my own children provided me with wonderful mermaids and spotted mythical beasts, far more expressive and exotic than I could possibly have imagined on my own!

Rusted, corroded and decaying objects and surfaces display interesting tones and textures for translation into abstract patterns and designs for rugs particularly. Aerial photography exposing the interesting shapes and textures of farmed and furrowed fields can also be the stimulus for abstract works.

Left: *Onion Studies*, 2011. Lynne Stein. Collage using stitched papers, raffia and thread.

Right: *Allotments*, 2012. Lynne Stein. Collage using stitched papers and photographic print.

None of the processes are restricted to creating purely two-dimensional or flat surfaces. Inspired perhaps by some of the flamboyant fashions on the catwalk, you might choose to embellish areas of knitwear using the latch-hooked technique or create decorative three-dimensional hand-hooked or tufted objects, ranging from birds and fertility dolls to a fancy gateau.

There is, of course, plenty of scope for creating functional objects using the techniques given, several examples being shown among the step-by-step projects (see pages 64–123). Durability may be a significant factor, and some techniques may be more appropriate than others, lending themselves to projects ranging from bolster cushions and doorstops to draught excluders.

Inspiration may be generated by a lucky find of fabrics or embellishment artefacts, which you feel compelled to incorporate. Unusual vintage buttons or a flamboyant floral fabric can frequently prompt my designs for a new creation! Being prepared to 'play' with a selection of fabrics and fibres of a chosen palette and being sensitive to their qualities in a fluid and highly intuitive way may lead to the development of a most interesting design, particularly in the case of handhooking and gun-tufting.

Above: *Bird*. Lynne Stein, 2008. 20 × 15 cm (8 × 6 in). Handhooked, beading, stitch. Mixed fabrics and fibres, wire, recycled buttons and beads. The three-dimensional form is created by the template shape, and the manner in which it is stitched.

If you are happy and relatively confident with drawing and painting materials, keeping a sketchbook is an ideal way of recording, developing and experimenting with ideas for your work. Of course, tracing and copying an image is also possible, and it is simple enough to reduce or enlarge a design. Needle punching lends itself to particularly graphic imagery, and I often find that making collages of my designs can be a more freeing preliminary process. Just as I store fabrics, I also salvage the colourful pages of glossy magazines, among other printed material, including my own photographic images, for this process. Additionally,

Left: *Wall Studies*, 2012. Lynne Stein. Reassembled and collaged cut and torn prints from the author's photograph collection.

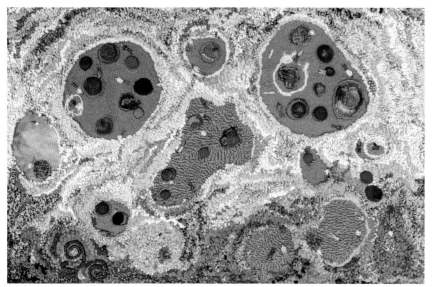

Left: *Divided We Fell* (Detail). Lynne Stein, 2021. Handhooked, needle punched, needle felted, appliquéd, stitched. Largely recycled fabrics and fibres, fleece, cotton thread and plastic. Based on the experience of succumbing to Covid, both on a personal and collective level.

keeping scrapbooks and creating mood boards, where colour schemes, embellishment details, fabric swatches, threads and yarns, backing cloth samples, photographs and mere doodles can all be registered, is of great value.

The internet provides an inexhaustible and invaluable source of information, both textual and visual, and as well as providing a wealth of interesting images, is also capable of helping you to solve logistical problems and locate suppliers for any of your textile-related needs. Digital photography, scanning and manipulation of your photographs with software such as Photoshop and various drawing and painting software programmes, along with the use of a handheld tablet, are extremely useful design aids. Many smartphones have good-quality integrated cameras, making recording and collating visual references a simple and direct procedure, and prompting the habit of seeking out aesthetically interesting objects and situations.

7 PROJECTS

ALLOTMENT VEGGIE MARKERS

This simple way to utilise and recycle shopping bags could be adapted to various vegetables and salad crops, and will be an instant reminder of sowing positions, as well as a bold and quirky way of jazzing up the veggie plot.

YOU WILL NEED:

- 45 cm (18 in) black woven polypropylene horticultural plastic
- Packaging tape
- Indelible white marker pen
- Quilting hoop
- Rug hook
- Plastic carrier bags: 4 orange, 3 dark green, 3 lime green – all cut into 1.5 cm (½ in) strips
- Scissors
- 45 cm (18 in) wire
- Needle
- Latex adhesive, spreader
- 2 small plastic storage crates with 25 × 14 cm (10 × 5 in) bases
- Indelible black marker pen
- 2 plastic-coated garden stakes
- Plastic-coated wire

Unless otherwise stated, all photographs in this chapter are © Robbie Wolfson.

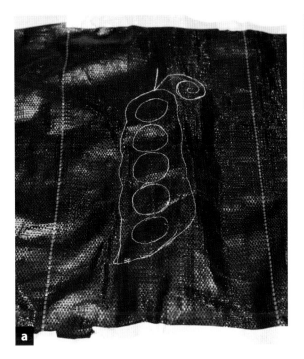

1 Cut the horticultural plastic in two, lengthways. Tape around all four sides of each piece, to prevent it from fraying.

2 Draw the carrot and pea-pod shapes onto each piece with your white marker (**a**).

3 Insert the carrot design sheet securely into your quilting hoop. Hook the entire shape finely and tightly so that it is very compact, making the loops of the green leaf shapes slightly longer (**b**). Shear the loops of the leaves so that there is textural contrast between the two areas (**c**). Take the design out of the hoop and set aside.

4 Insert the pea-pod design sheet into your hoop. Again, hook the whole design very tightly, working on the circular lime-green pea shapes first.

5 Remove the design from the hoop, trimming the excess plastic to 2.5 cm (1 in) beyond the outer edge of the hooked shape and snipping it close to the hooking line at intervals (**d**). Working from the front of the design, fold behind the excess plastic and stitch carefully in place, ensuring that the shape is precise.

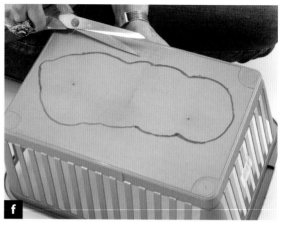

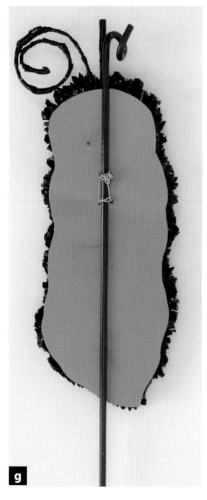

6 To make one of the tendrils, fold 15 cm (6 in) of wire double and wrap it tightly with a long strip of dark green plastic (see Techniques, page 43), securing the end by threading it back through the inside of the wrapped tube (**e**).

7 To make the thinner spiral stem, repeat this process, using only a single 30 cm (12 in) length of wire. Once the wire is bound with the plastic and secured, bend it into a spiral.

8 Attach both wrapped wire pieces to the back of the pea pod, by stitching them securely into position, again working from the front so that none of your hooking is dislodged.

9 Repeat Step 5 with the carrot. Spread latex on the reverse side of both shapes and allow to dry.

10 Cut the bases from the plastic crates, and draw with the black marker around your carrot and pea-pod templates on each (**f**). Cut these out with heavy-duty scissors. At the upper centre of both shapes, pierce four holes to form a rectangle accommodating the width of the stakes.

11 Spread latex thinly across the top of both bases and press each hooked shape on top, carefully lining them up. Allow to dry.

12 Thread the plastic-coated wire onto a sharp needle, stitching carefully through the pierced holes and hooked surfaces, and securing the veggie markers to the stakes by knotting them tightly at the back several times (**g**).

CHRISTMAS STOCKING

Roomy enough for those foil-wrapped tangerines, as well as the more precious presents, this will become an heirloom piece for passing from one generation to the next.

YOU WILL NEED:

- Tracing paper
- Pencil
- Transfer pencil
- Pins
- Hessian (approx. 72 cm/28 in square)
- Iron, pressing cloth
- Frame
- Drawing pins or staple gun and staples
- Indelible marker
- Assorted fabrics, cut into long strips, 1.5 cm (½ in) wide
- Rug hook
- Small amount of pink fleece
- Felting needle, size 36/38
- Felting sponge
- Flexible wire or scoobies
- Pink and brown yarns
- Buttons, beads, toy eyes, silver bell, buckle
- Scissors
- Latex adhesive, spreader
- Large piece of felt, 56 cm (22 in) square
- Bodkin, needles, thread
- Green braided piping cord, 137 cm (54 in)

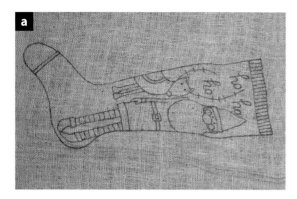

1   Draw the 48 × 28 cm (19 × 11 in) stocking shape onto tracing paper. Reversing the paper, draw over the design with a transfer pencil. Pin the paper, transfer side face down, onto your hessian. Keeping both hessian and paper flat, cover them with a cloth and go over the design with a hot iron, transferring the image onto the hessian. Remove the paper and clarify the image with a marker (**a**). Attach the hessian tightly onto a frame, ensuring that the design is positioned centrally and not distorted.

2   Using a sturdy fabric such as felted knitwear for the background, start hooking, pulling the loops to a height of 5 mm (¼ in).

3   The lettering should be hooked using black stretchy material, such as tights.

4   Santa's beard can be hooked in knitwear, varying the loop height to maximise texture, and his cheeks hooked in wool, shearing the loops.

5   Using a felting needle and pink fleece (see Techniques, page 49) shape Santa's nose (**b**).

6   Work the reindeer's antlers by wire wrapping with woollen yarn (see Techniques, page 43), securing them by couching with the same wool (**c**).

7   Stitch the bell, nose, lace trim, buckle, eye beads and buttons in place (**d**).

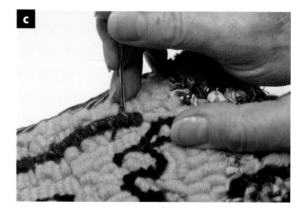

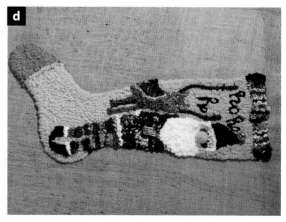

8   Unpin the hessian and cut out the stocking, leaving a 2.5 cm (1 in) border around it.

9   Snip the border close to the hooking line at intervals, folding the overlap back on the reverse, and stitching it in place from the front (**e**). Spread latex thinly, covering the reverse of the stocking. Leave to dry overnight.

10 Using the stocking as your template, cut two additional shapes out of felt. Use the first piece for lining the hooked stocking and the second for lining the stocking's back (**f**).

11 Cut out a slightly larger duplicate shape for the stocking's back from a sturdy and suitably coloured fabric, leaving an additional seam allowance. Stitch a hem at the top.

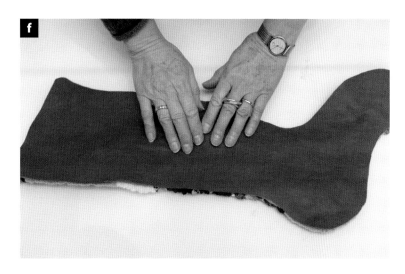

12 Stitch the second felt lining shape to the reverse of the stocking's back. Turning in the seam allowance, stitch the stocking's back to the hooked front, adjusting the shape to fit.

13 Apply latex to each end and allow it to dry, then stitch the piping cord around the stocking's edge (**g**), concealing the ends inside the stocking and leaving enough at the right side for a hanging loop.

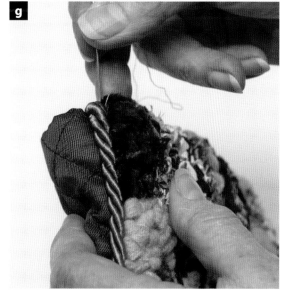

CIRCULAR SEAT PAD

Cosy and tactile, this latch-hooked piece can be used at home either
as a stool cushion or a wall decoration.

YOU WILL NEED:

- Pencil, transfer pencil
- Tracing paper
- White card, A2 sheet
- Masking tape
- Indelible marker
- Magazine/coloured paper cuttings (optional)
- Cellophane
- Stiff card, 13 cm (5 in) length
- Rug gauge

- Latch-hook rug canvas, 50 x 50 cm (20 x 20 in)
- Latch hook
- Needle, linen thread
- Assortment of yarns with different types, tones and textures, including gold, amber and variegated dyes
- Scissors
- Rug binding tape, 1 m (39 in)
- Fabric for lining, 50 x 50 cm (20 x 20 in)

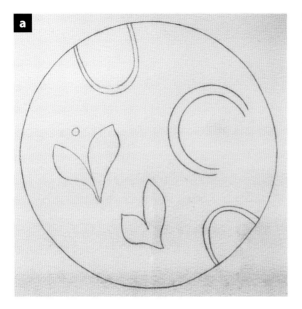

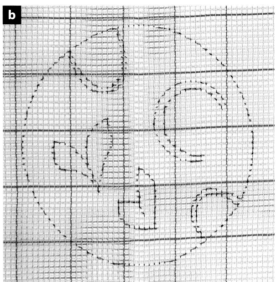

1 Draw a 33 cm- (13 in-) diameter circle onto a sheet of tracing paper, marking the design within the circle. Reverse the paper and draw over the design with a transfer pencil. Draw the 33 cm- (13 in-) diameter circle on a sheet of white card, then turn the tracing paper over again and place it on top of this circle outline. Draw over the traced outlines and lift the tracing paper to reveal your basic design on the card (**a**).

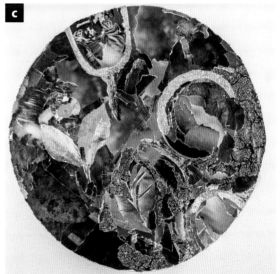

2 Tape around the raw edges of the rug canvas to keep them intact while working on the piece. Place your rug canvas on top of the card and trace the design with an indelible marker (**b**).

3 As a useful colour reference, you can create a collage on your sheet of card using magazine cuttings and papers (**c**). Cover the finished collage with a sheet of cellophane, taped around the back to secure it.

4 Use a 13 cm (5 in) length of stiff card as your rug gauge for cutting the yarn for the majority of the design (**d**), and a standard rug gauge for preparing shorter lengths of yarn to fill certain marked shapes, to be worked in gold and amber.

5 Apart from the defined shapes, this design is worked in a very 'free-form' way, relying on the shifting tones and textures of your yarns. The variegated yarns will give it extra richness (**e**).

6 Begin by latch hooking part of the outer area (see Techniques, page 47) (**f**). If the yarn you are using is not too thick, you can easily use two strands together.

7 The curved linear shapes can be worked in amber wool and a mixture of gold yarns (**g**). Take care to follow the shapes' outlines. You will notice that this is creating a lower-level pile.

8 Work around the outer surface of these shapes, combining your yarns to create interesting tonal blends, and ensuring that the surface of the rug canvas is sufficiently filled to give the work a full and slightly bevelled appearance (**h**).

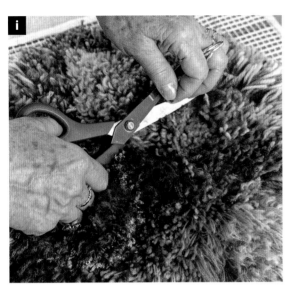

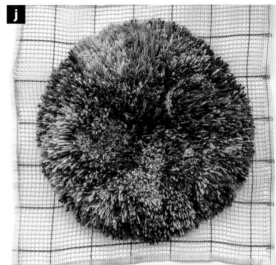

9 While maintaining the shaggy, tactile quality of the piece, carefully trim any areas as necessary (**i**), to emphasise and clarify the overall design.

10 Cut around the design, leaving a 2.5 cm (1 in) surplus of rug canvas (**j**). Turn the work over, folding the excess canvas inwards as you work your way around the circle, pressing little folded pleats as you go.

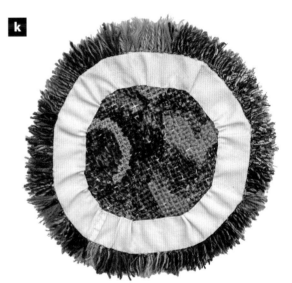

11 Fold and stitch the raw edge of the binding. Working along the circumference of the piece, carefully stitch one side of the binding to the canvas, connecting them as closely as possible to the last hooked knot all the way around, and flattening the pleats underneath. Fold and stitch the other overlapping raw edge of the binding and stitch the ends together (**k**).

12 Starting at the join in the tape, create a running stitch with a long length of doubled thread around the inner edge of the binding, easing it flatter by gently pulling the thread. Carefully stitch this edge of the binding to the canvas.

13 Cut out a circle of lining fabric, slightly bigger than the reverse surface area to be covered. Turning the lining's outer edge under, hem stitch around it, connecting it to the binding tape (**l**).

EMBROIDERY HOOP PORTRAIT

A funky punch needle project using fabric and yarns to create a colourful character which will enhance any child's nursery or bedroom wall.

YOU WILL NEED:

- Linen foundation fabric for punch needle, 50 cm (20 in)
- Chalk
- Fine indelible marker
- Morgan no-slip quilting hoop, 30 cm (12 in)
- Oxford punch needle, size 10 regular
- Range of yarns in appropriate colours and thicknesses, including rug, tapestry, knitting and crewel wool
- Finely patterned cotton fabric strips, 1 cm (½ in) wide
- Embroidery scissors
- Lavor fine punch needle and threader
- 2 shirt buttons
- Needles, threads
- Scissors
- Latex, spreader
- Wooden embroidery hoop, 25 cm (10 in)
- Linen thread
- All-purpose adhesive, fine applicator
- Mini pom-pom braid, 1 m (39 in)
- Patterned narrow ribbon, 33 cm (13 in)
- Plain narrow ribbon, 10 cm (4 in)
- Tape measure

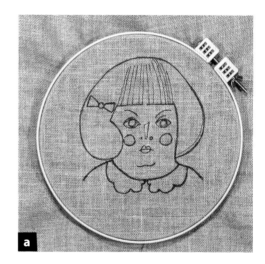

1 Draw a portrait in the centre of your piece of linen with chalk, ensuring that it will eventually fit within the smaller wooden embroidery frame. When you are satisfied with the features, go over them with your marker, emphasising the lips more heavily so that they will register on the reverse of the cloth when held up to the light. Position your linen centrally within the quilting frame, ensuring that it is sufficiently taut (**a**).

2   Thread your Oxford punch needle with two-ply rug wool. Start to fill in the skin area of the face (**b**), working gradually and in sections around the shapes of the cheeks and other features (**c**).

3   With a suitable yarn, use the same punch needle to fill in the hair (**d**), leaving the outline of the bow unfilled at this stage. Use darker contrasting tones along the drawn lines within the fringe and any other area of the hair you wish to emphasise.

4   In your chosen colour, fill in the shapes of the girl's collar, maintaining its curved outlines (**e**).

5   For textural contrast, thread your Oxford needle with a long strip of fabric, and repeating this as necessary, work the remainder of the girl's top, leaving an irregular line at the bottom (**f**).

6   Turning the work over, carefully fill in the lips so that the loops will appear on the front surface. Turn the work over again to the right side, and sculpt the lips to the desired shape using your embroidery scissors (**g**).

7 Use your threader to load the fine Lavor punch needle, with fine crewel wool for the nose, chin and eye areas (**h**). A sparkly yarn can enhance the eyes (**i**).

8 Stitch the two buttons into place, using a sharp needle (**j**).

9 When most of the hair has been filled, work the bow area in a different direction with your punch needle, so that its shape will be distinguishable. Create a bow with your length of ribbon, and stitch this in place (**k**).

10 Take the work out of the quilting frame. Turning it over, trim all loose ends of fabric and yarns, and spread the reverse surface carefully with a thin layer of latex. Leave to dry.

11 Transfer the work to the smaller wooden embroidery hoop. To ensure the work remains taut, temporarily oversew it with linen thread at several places around the circumference of the frame, to hold it in place (**l**).

12 Using an all-purpose adhesive, glue around opposite sections of the hoop with a fine applicator (**m**). Stretch the cloth taut as you stick it down, removing your stitches, and allowing areas to dry before proceeding to the next part.

13 Once the work is completely dry, cut away all surplus foundation fabric on the reverse side so that it is flush with the hoop. Apply glue very thinly along the edge of the fabric to prevent fraying (**n**).

14 Tucking under and gluing one end of your pom-pom braid, glue the required length around the outer hoop, tucking the other end under also (**o**).

15 Once this has dried, place it over the inner hoop, ensuring that the clasp is placed centrally over the work. Tighten the screw at the top to secure the whole piece. Finish by threading ribbon through the clasp, so your work is ready to be hung (**p**).

FLORAL TOTE BAG

Decorated with an array of colourful needle-punched flowers, this is a perfect tote for a trip to the florist or farmers' market.

YOU WILL NEED:

- Sheet of thin white card
- Pencil
- Paper scissors, fabric scissors
- Jute tote bag – lightweight, unlined, coloured
- Newspaper sheets
- Indelible black marker pens: thin and heavy
- Square plastic snap frame, 28 cm (11 in)
- Oxford punch needle, size 14
- Lavor punch needle
- Punch needle threader
- Variety of woollen and acrylic yarns in different colours
- Napping shears, embroidery scissors
- Plastic bag
- Latex adhesive, spreader

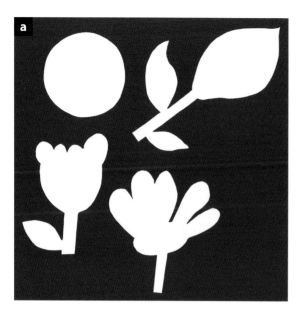

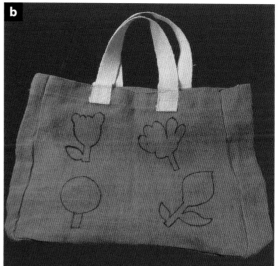

1 Draw your flower templates onto thin card and cut them out carefully (**a**).

2 Insert several sheets of newspaper to separate the sides of the bag, then draw around each template on one side of the bag with a thin indelible marker. Go over the shapes with a thicker black indelible marker so they will be easily visible on their reverse side (**b**). Repeat the process on the other side, changing the configuration of flower shapes, if you choose.

3 Turn the bag inside out, and draw over the exposed lines, so that the designs are clear on both sides.

4 Keeping the bag inside out, insert the plastic snap frame into it (**c**).

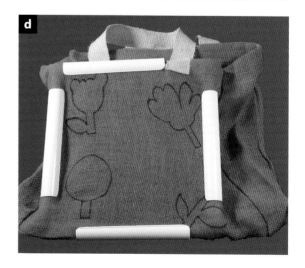

5 Close the fastening clips around each side so that the jute fabric is taut and at least one of the flowers is in position for being needle punched (**d**). Although some of the flower stems could be contrastingly flat 'embroidery' stitch and worked from the front, the majority of the shapes should be worked from their reverse sides, showing their looped surfaces on the front of the bag.

6 Thread the size 14 Oxford punch needle with your chosen yarn. Start to work your first shape, aiming to create a fairly closely packed flat 'embroidery' stitch (**e**). You can create textural variety with your choice of yarns, size of punch needle, and direction and spacing of your needle punching (**f**).

7 Napping shears and embroidery scissors are useful for achieving a satisfying sculptural shape with a dense, velvety pile (**g**).

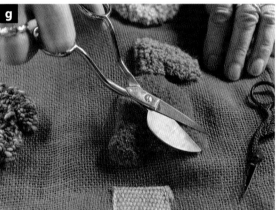

8 Undo the frame and repeat Steps 4 and 5, repositioning the bag to expose the area you are working.

9 When you have completed one side of the bag, turn it inside out, and lay a plastic bag between the two sides. Thinly spread latex adhesive on the reverse of each flower. Repeat on the other side once the first side is dry. Once dry, turn it inside out again to admire (**h**)!

FLOWER POWER GARLAND

This idea can also be adapted for a Christmas wreath, using different fabrics and colours, and perhaps substituting the butterfly with cinnamon sticks and candy canes for more of a seasonal feel. The individual flowers could make a lovely brooch or corsage. Several different floral-patterned fabrics – all charity shop finds – have been selected for maximum effect.

YOU WILL NEED:

- Metal coat hanger
- Frame
- Lime-green patterned cotton fabrics, cut into 10 × 2.5 cm (4 × 1 in) pieces
- Scissors
- Hessian to fit
- Colourful and floral fabrics, cut into 7.5 × 2.5 cm (3 × 1 in) pieces
- 92 cm (1 yd) checked nylon

- ribbon, cut into 6.5 cm (2½ in) pieces
- 1 square of yellow felt, cut into 6.5 × 2 cm (2½ × ¾ in) pieces
- Prodder
- Brown and beige woollen yarns
- White net, 45 cm (18 in)
- Fabric markers
- Latex adhesive, spreader

- 3 coloured buttons
- Felting needle, size 36/38
- Felting sponge
- Brown and red unspun fleece, small amounts
- Needles, threads
- Rug hook
- 14 small dark beads, 2 small silver beads
- Nylon wire

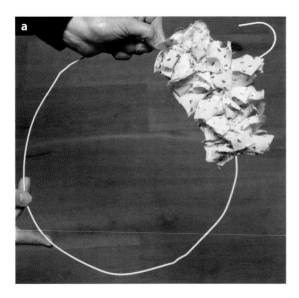

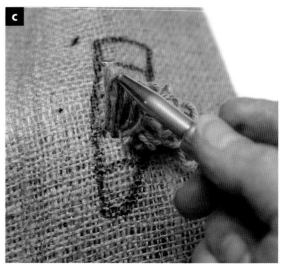

1 Bend the coat hanger into a circle, retaining the hook for hanging. Work the green fabric strips in a closely packed row around your circle, tying each tightly with a simple knot to secure, and leaving the hook uncovered (**a**). Trim any irregularities to maintain a pleasing shape.

2 On your stretched hessian, draw six well-spaced circles with an indelible marker, ranging from 2.5 (1 in) to 5 cm (2 in) in diameter. Additionally, draw the shape of a butterfly body.

3 Selecting combinations of fabrics to give each flower a different colour, work each of the circles with your prodder, starting from the outside of each and packing your prodding quite tightly, working towards the centres (**b**).

4 Using at least four strands of yarn simultaneously, hook the butterfly's body, alternating the beige and brown stripes and leaving your loops considerably longer and packed tightly together (**c**). This should be sheared and sculpted with sharp scissors (see Techniques, page 43).

5 Scribble across your net fabric with fabric markers, leaving enough of its natural colour exposed (see Embellishments, page 51). Cut the net into 10 × 2.5 cm (4 × 1 in) pieces (**d**), and hook enough of these along each side of the butterfly's body to resemble its wings. Trim them to further define their shape.

6 Cut out each circle leaving an overlap of 1.5 cm (½ in), which should be stitched in place on the reverse and spread with a thin layer of latex. Treat the butterfly shape in the same way. Leave to dry.

7 Turn the circles over and trim to define satisfactory floral shapes (**e**). Sew buttons in the centres of three flowers.

8 With your felting needle, sponge and red fleece, create a small spherical shape to be stitched in to the centre of one of the other flowers (see Techniques, page 49).

9 Also with your needle-felting tools, create a small brown head for the butterfly. Stitch this to the top of the body, applying silver beads for its eyes, and small dark beads threaded onto nylon wire, for its antennae (**f**).

10 Stitch strong thread through the reverse of each individual shape, and tie tightly into their required positions around the garland (**g**). Trim any excess threads on the reverse.

FRIED EGG POT HOLDER

This bold graphic design is a witty way of ensuring that you don't burn your fingers when cooking the breakfast!

1 Draw your fried egg shape on the hessian, making the outer circle slightly irregular.

2 Insert the hessian into your hoop, ensuring that it is sufficiently taut.

3 Begin by hooking the entire egg yolk shape at the centre, keeping your loops as compact and even as possible.

4 Hook closely around this with white T-shirt fabric, maintaining the same appearance (**a**).

5 When the whole shape is filled in, remove it from the hoop and trim around the design, leaving an excess of 2.5 cm (1 in).

YOU WILL NEED:

- Hessian
- Indelible marker
- Bowls or plates for circular templates, 25 and 9 cm (10 and 3½ in) radius
- Quilting hoop
- Rug hook
- Yellow towelling fabric, 25 cm (10 in) radius circle plus 5 mm (¼ in) overlap
- White and yellow T-shirt fabric, cut into 1.5 cm (½ in) strips
- Wide-eyed needle, needles and threads, pins
- Scissors
- Latex adhesive, spreader
- White lining fabric, two 25 cm (10 in) radius circles plus 5 mm (¼ in) overlap
- Colour coordinated ribbon, 15 cm (6 in) length
- Domette interlining fabric or heat resistant batting, two circles to fit

6 Turn the excess to the reverse side of the design and tack it in place from the front. Lightly latex over the raw edge of the hessian and leave to dry (**b**).

7 With a long strip of the white fabric, oversew to bind the outer shape of the fried egg (**c**).

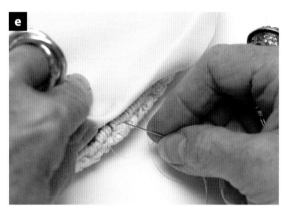

8 Sandwich a circle of Domette interlining fabric between the reverse of the fried egg shape and a circle of the lining fabric (**d**), and hem the lining in place (**e**).

9 Likewise, sandwich Domette between the towelling and lining circles and hem into place (**f**).

10 Place the fried egg shape over the towelling circle, with the lining fabrics facing each other on the inside. Neatly oversew the two shapes together, leaving an opening of a comfortable handspan. Insert the folded ribbon loop opposite the opening and stitch into place (**g**).

HAIR ACCESSORIES

The template for each hair decoration is a very simple shape, and each can be hooked or prodded on a quilting hoop. I have included delicate sequined fabrics, metallic lurex and ribbons to achieve the glitzy effect in each, but you may wish to use entirely different fabrics for these pieces. The ideas could be scaled up or down in size, made into brooches, or stitched as decorations for pull-on hats, bags or pockets.

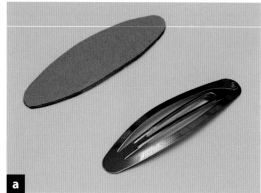

YOU WILL NEED:

- Alice band, hair comb, hair clip
- Card
- Scissors
- Hessian, 45 cm (18 in)
- Quilting hoop
- Woollen knitwear and assorted fabrics
- Extra-fine rug hook
- Latex adhesive, spreader
- Felt or wool, small piece
- Needles, pins, strong thread
- Pencil, ruler, indelible marker
- 8 cm- (3 in-) diameter circular object
- Felting needle, size 36/38
- Felting sponge
- Sequins

Hair clip

1 Cut an oval card template, slightly bigger than the outer shape of your hair clip (**a**). With your marker, draw around this on the hessian, and insert it in your quilting hoop, ensuring that it is taut, for ease of hooking.

2 Hook the shape with narrow strips of sequinned fabric.

3 Cut out the finished shape, leaving a 1.5 cm (½ in) border. Tuck in the overlap on the reverse of the work and stitch this in place, working from the front.

4 Spread latex on the reverse side to dry overnight.

5 Line the reverse with felt or woollen cloth and stitch the hair clip securely in place (**b**).

Hair comb

1 Cut a rectangular card template measuring 8 × 5 cm (3 × 2 in), or slightly broader than your comb. Cut a heart template to fit within the shape.

2 Draw around these on the hessian, placing the heart centrally within the rectangle. Insert the hessian in your quilting hoop (**a**).

3 Hook the rectangular shape with narrow strips of stretchy lurex, working around the heart shape.

4 Hook the heart shape with narrow gold ribbon, carefully shearing the loops once you have completed the shape.

5 Repeat the same finishing process as previously (**b**), finally stitching the rectangular shape onto the comb (**c**).

© Joel Stein

Alice band

1 Using an 8 cm- (3 in-) diameter object as your template, draw the circular shape onto your hessian. Insert the hessian into your quilting hoop.

2 Hook the shape in concentric circles using a combination of 1.5 cm- (½ in-) wide strips of recycled woollen knitwear, and decorative ribbons. Leave your loops slightly longer towards the outer edge. Trim them all, sculpting the whole shape.

3 Cut a long 1.5 cm- (½ in-) wide strip of knitwear and wind it around your finger into a tight sphere. Use a felting needle to perfect its shape.

4 Sew this into the centre of your circular shape, decorating it with a few stitched sequins (**a**).

5 Take a long 2.5 cm (1 in) strip of knitwear fabric and bind the Alice band tightly in a diagonal direction (**b**), stitching it at each end.

6 Repeat the same finishing processes as for the other hair accessories and stitch your circle securely into an off-centre position on your Alice band.

a

b

'HOME IS WHERE THE HEARTS ARE!'

This draught excluder is made using a locker hook needle, which gives it a particularly sturdy and durable quality. Although a more time-consuming project, it is easily portable, and can be made with minimal expense while watching TV!

YOU WILL NEED:

- Coloured pencils, paper, tracing paper, dressmaker's carbon paper, thin card
- Indelible marker
- Scissors
- 45 cm (18 in) of 1m (40 in) wide rug canvas (three holes to 1 in)
- Assorted needles, dressmaker's pins
- Assorted durable fabrics, including felt, T-shirts, velour
- Rug yarn, strong twine, cotton
- Locker hook needle
- Lining material, 96 × 25 cm (38 × 10 in)
- 2.7 m (3 yd) mini pom-pom braid
- 91 cm (36 in) draught excluder inner pad
- Backing fabric 107 × 38 cm (42 × 15 in)
- 3 press studs

a

1 Within an outer rectangle 22 × 94 cm (8½ × 37 in), trace your design from its original drawing, using card templates for the hearts and letters if necessary (**a**). Use alternative fonts if preferred. Transfer the traced design directly onto the rug canvas using dressmaker's carbon paper. Clarify the design with a marker pen (**b**).

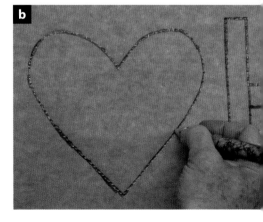

b

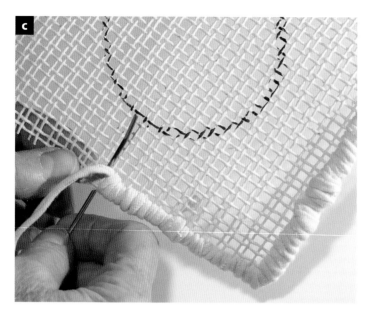

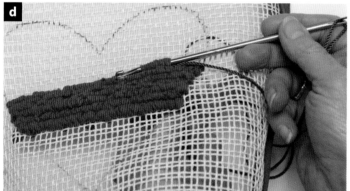

2 Folding under the surplus edges of your canvas, bind the outer edges of the design by oversewing them with a carpet needle and T-shirt fabric strips in the background colour, so that the stitches overlap and the corners are mitred (**c**).

3 Cut long fabric strips in 2 cm (¾ in) widths, depending on their quality and thickness, aiming to cover the rug canvas mesh and holes.

4 Thread a good length of rug yarn through the eye of your locker hook needle. Holding your fabric strip underneath the canvas, use the forefinger of your other hand to poke the hooked part of the locker needle through a hole, catching a loop of the fabric from underneath and pulling it up through the canvas (see Techniques, page 41). Work from right to left, trying to ensure that your loops are even (**d**).

5 Hook approximately ten loops at a time onto your needle, pulling it through the loops so that the yarn anchors them in place (**e**). Repeat this process until each shape is filled in with the appropriate colour, including the paler background area.

6 Turn your finished design over and lay your lining fabric on top of the reverse, turning under the raw edges. Neatly slip stitch the lining in place around all four sides of the design (**f**).

7 Stitch the pom-pom braid around the entire outer edge of the design's front surface (**g**).

8 Turning under the raw edges of your backing fabric, create a 2.5 cm- (1 in-) width double-turn hem along one of the short ends. Neatly slip stitch the other three sides to the bound edges of the rug canvas, inserting the cushion pad before you finish stitching the third side.

9 Stitch the press studs in place in evenly spaced corresponding positions along both inner sides of the cover (**h**).

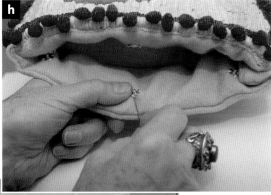

HOOKED AND BRAIDED RUG

Combining two traditional rug-making techniques as well as decorative embellishment, this rug is both pretty and practical.

YOU WILL NEED:

Hooked area:

- Tracing paper, transfer pencil, ruler
- 92 cm (1 yd) hessian
- Needles, strong thread, black cotton thread, pins
- Pressing cloth, iron
- Indelible marker, pencil
- Rug frame, trestles
- Assorted non-fraying fabrics, ribbons and yarns
- Scissors
- Rug hook
- Button
- Dyed fleece, assorted colours, small amounts
- Felting needle, size 36/38
- Felting sponge
- Latex, spreader
- 92 cm (1 yd) hessian or lining fabric

Braided border:

- 3 flat woollen fabrics, each 264 × 5 cm (104 × 2 in) wide
- Tape measure, ruler
- Scissors or rotary cutter and mat
- Carpet needle
- Large kilt safety pin

1 Draw the design for the hooked part of the rug onto tracing paper, within its outer measurement of 77 × 52 cm (30 × 20½ in). Reverse the paper and draw over the design with a transfer pencil. Pin the paper transfer side down onto the hessian, keeping both surfaces flat. Cover with a cloth and go over the design with a hot iron, transferring the image onto the hessian. Remove the paper and clarify the image with your marker.

2 Attach the hessian onto your frame with strong thread, and mount the frame onto a pair of trestles (**a**) (see Preparation, page 38).

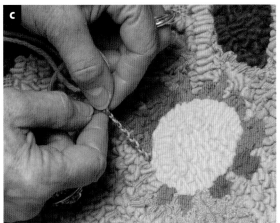

3 Using various green fabrics for the foliage, bright colours for the flowers and sun, and glittery fabric for the flower stamens, use a contrasting blend of closely toned fabrics for the background.

4 Shear the loops on some of the stems (**b**), and hook the small flowers with colourful ribbon for textural contrast.

5 Once you have hooked the sun, secure three strands of woollen yarn to the outer edge of the circle, braiding and then couching them to form an outline (**c**). Secure any excess threads through the rug's reverse.

6 The animal should be hooked using closely toned fabrics, highlighting with printed fabric and colour co-ordinated yarns for the spots (**d**). Stitch a button with black thread for the eye.

7 For additional flowers, needle felt small spherical shapes in toning colours (**e**) (see Techniques, page 49). Stitch a smaller shape on top of the larger one (**f**), stitching them through the rug.

8　Once the hooking is completed, cut your braiding fabrics into strips 5 cm (2 in) wide, giving them as much length as possible. If the lengths are shorter than 1.8 m (2 yd), sew them end to end, creating neat 5 mm (¼ in) seams. However, to avoid bulky and uneven braids, try to stagger the position of your seams occurring in the same positions of your fabrics. You will need total lengths of 4.5 m (5 yd). Your fabric strips should be rolled up and pinned to avoid becoming tangled as you braid (**g**).

9　Fasten three strips together to the large safety pin, attaching this to a static object, such as a cup hook or handle, positioned slightly above eye level. Begin braiding the strips close to the pin (see Techniques, page 44), trying to maintain an even tension, and ensuring that any raw edges are turned to the back as the braiding progresses (**h**). As the made braid length increases, tie it together and set it to your left, as you work.

10　Once you have achieved the necessary length of braid, remove the safety pin, secure the loose ends with a pin and sew each end, tapering the braid and neatly tucking in any raw edges.

11　Keeping sufficient hessian surplus beyond your hooking, stitch the braid around the perimeter of the hooked rug, sewing edge to edge and occasionally through the braid and the hessian surplus, with tiny stitches to maintain its position (**i**).

12　Turning the rug over, fold the surplus hessian under, so that it is just within the braid's edge, mitring corners and carefully stitching at necessary intervals (**j**). Spread a thin layer of latex across the hooked area, and allow to dry overnight. Turning a small amount under on all sides, stitch your lining or hessian neatly to the rug's reverse.

'IT'S A WRAP!'

This decorative piece of wall art is made almost entirely from chocolate biscuit wrappers and other recycled packaging and household items. Most of the embellishments could also be junk shop finds.

YOU WILL NEED:

- Indelible marker, ruler
- Stretched artist's canvas 40 × 30 cm (16 × 12 in)
- Hessian to fit
- Frame
- 2 beer bottle tops
- Coloured sequins, large flat beads, smaller round beads
- Plastic bath scrubs and packaging offcuts
- Assorted threads and small fabric remnants
- Iron, old towels
- Printed foil chocolate and biscuit wrappers
- Scissors
- Rug hook
- Black plastic bin liners, coloured and white plastic bags
- Plastic mesh fruit bags
- Latex adhesive, spreader, all-purpose adhesive
- Assorted safety pins
- Drawing pins or staple gun and staples
- Non-stick baking parchment

1 Stretch and pin or staple your hessian onto your frame. With an indelible marker, draw a rectangle on your hessian, measuring the same dimensions as your artist's canvas. Divide the design into three areas, drawing a row of uneven lateral stripes within the left rectangle, and either freehand or with a card template, draw the floral shapes within the right rectangle (**a**).

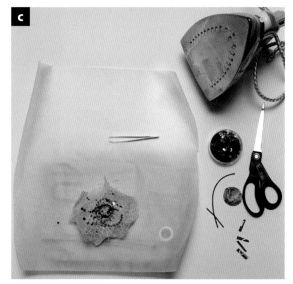

2 Arrange your embellishment artefacts within the middle rectangle, and draw around these shapes. One inverted bottle top should encase one of the large flat beads, while the other can be flattened with a hammer to expose its design (**b**). Set these aside.

3 From an assortment of plastic bath scrubs, sequins, threads, and small plastic offcuts and fabric remnants, create areas of colourful heat-bonded plastics (**c**) (see Embellishments, page 51).

4 Using the same bonding process, treat areas of hooked printed foil packaging on hessian in the same way. These can be cut into specific floral shapes, such as flower centres and petals, and a circular spiral shape, to be placed within your design and glued with an all-purpose adhesive (**d**) before hooking the surrounding area.

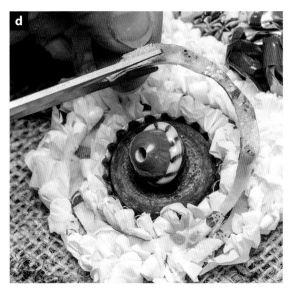

5 With a selection of printed foil packaging for the area on the left, hook each stripe or subdivision in a different colour (**e**).

6 Using strips of white plastic 5 mm (¼ in) wide, hook the middle panel, working around and omitting the drawn shapes.

7 Fill in the floral forms within the right rectangle, with a mixture of cut heat-bonded areas and hooked strips of coloured plastic carrier bags, bath scrubs and mesh fruit bags (**f**). Some areas can be sheared or cut to create more textural contrast. Hook the background, carefully defining each shape, using narrow strips of black plastic bin liner.

8 Using all-purpose adhesive, attach the embellishment artefacts within the white hooked panel, piling smaller beads on top of the larger flat ones, and positioning the circular plastic spiral around the encased bead (**g**).

9 Once these are dry, stitch safety pins in place to resemble flower petals around the bottle top.

10 Unpinning the hessian from your frame, cut around the outer edge of the design, leaving a 2.5 cm (1 in) overlap. Turning the excess hessian to the back, stitch from the front, ensuring that there is no surplus hessian showing.

11 Trim any loose ends on the reverse, then spread latex evenly across the whole surface, and also across the canvas (**h**). Positioning the hooked design carefully onto the canvas, so that the edges line up, stick the two surfaces together, leaving to dry overnight.

LADY TEA COSY

Afternoon teas are back in fashion, and along with the finger sandwiches and cupcakes, this characterful tea cosy will add warmth and humour to any table and teapot!

YOU WILL NEED:

- Frame
- 2 pieces hessian to fit
- Card
- Pencil, chalk, indelible marker
- Drawing pins or staple gun and staples
- Assorted smooth fabrics, cut into 1.5 cm (½ in) strips
- Rug hook
- Scissors
- Small amount red knitted fabric, cut into 1.5 cm (½ in) strips
- Needles, threads, pins
- 1 small black button, 1 larger green button
- Latex adhesive, spreader
- Wadding (batting), 45 cm (18 in)
- Lining fabric, 45 cm (18 in)
- 23 cm (9 in) woven mohair, cut into long strips
- Tights

1 Attach the hessian tightly to your frame. Draw the outer tea cosy shape, either freehand or with the aid of a card template, onto the centre of your hessian with an indelible marker, ensuring it measures 35.5 × 28 cm (14 × 11 in). You will need to repeat this process on a second piece of stretched hessian once the front has been hooked, to create the tea cosy's back.

2 Fill in the details of both designs freehand or with templates for the different features (**a**).

3 Using different tones of yellow and ochre fabrics, hook the hair, varying the widths of the stripes (**b**).

4 Hook the hat in bright colours that differ from the rest of the project's palette, hooking the band of the hat in lateral lines (**c**).

5 With red knitted fabric for the mouth, shear and sculpt the longer hooked loops to emphasise this feature (**d**) (see Techniques, page 43).

6 Work the cheeks in concentric circles of bright pink material, and the face in flesh-coloured fabric.

7 Hook one eye in green, and combine a small black button and a larger green one for the other.

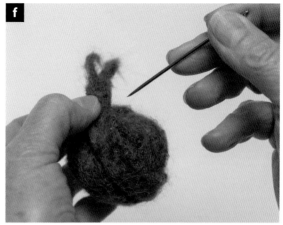

8 Taking care to position the hat line accurately, the tea cosy's back should be hooked similarly, matching the front's colours.

9 When finished, detach from the frame and cut around both shapes, leaving an overlap of 2.5 cm (1 in). Repeat Steps 6 and 8 of the fried egg pot holder project (see page 84), leaving 1.5 cm (½ in) of the hessian exposed around the sides of each shape, apart from their straight bases (**e**).

10 Cut two template shapes of wadding, making them 1.5 cm (½ in) smaller, inserting a layer between the reverse of each tea cosy shape and the lining fabric. Turn in a 1.5 cm (½ in) hem and stitch the lining in place.

11 Sew the two shapes together with strong thread, filling any gaps by overstitching with appropriate colours of fabric.

12 Cut your mohair into long enough 2.5 cm- (1 in-) width strips to wind tightly into a 7.5 cm (3 in) diameter sphere, needle felting it a little to define its shape (**f**). Knot it inside an old pair of tights and felt it in the washing machine, on a hot cycle (see Embellishments, page 51).

13 Remove the tights, and when dry, stitch the pom-pom to the top of the hat with a double length of woollen yarn. Note that If the mohair is dye-fast, you may wish to create several pom-poms simultaneously, in this way, for future projects.

LAZY DAISY CHAIN

A pretty addition to your wardrobe, this necklace is inexpensive and simple to make, and a fine example of inventive recycling.

YOU WILL NEED:

- 45 cm (18 in) hessian
- Quilting hoop
- Orange, pink and red bouclé yarn
- Fine pencil rug hook
- Scissors
- 7 flexible plastic juice carton tops, 2.5 cm (1 in) diameter
- Knitting wool, contrasting colours
- 'Jewels' or beads
- Needles, thread
- Latex adhesive, thin spreader
- 92 cm (1 yd) coloured twisted paper string
- Assorted colour co-ordinated (vintage) buttons
- Fine indelible marker pen

1 According to the length of necklace you require, use a template to draw six or seven 2.5 cm (1 in) diameter circles onto your hessian with your marker pen.

2 Insert the hessian into your hoop, ensuring that it is sufficiently taut.

3 Starting from the centre of each circle, hook the shapes tightly (**a**), making two of each colour, using the orange, pink and red bouclé yarns.

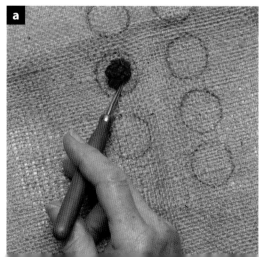

4 Carefully cut each shape out, leaving a very small overlap in the hessian around them (**b**), and checking their fit within your carton top.

5 Decorate each hooked circle with contrasting wool, sewing diagonal lines that intersect at the middle.

6 Stitch a bead or diamante 'jewel' at the centre of each circle (**c**), slightly tightening as you secure it, to maintain the detail.

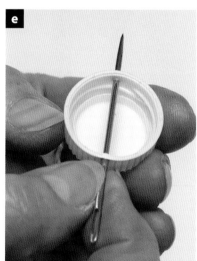

7 Immediately latex the sides and reverse of each (**d**), and leave to dry.

8 Pierce two opposite sides of each carton top with a tapestry needle (**e**), and thread paper string through these holes, interspersing each cap with a few threaded coloured buttons.

9 Spread more latex onto the reverse of each circle, and press each into place within the tops. The detail of each daisy can be redefined by manipulating the loops and decoration with the eye of your needle.

10 Deciding on the required length of your necklace, thread a button onto one end of the string, securing with a knot, and create an appropriately sized knotted loop at the other end to fasten.

MIZZY-MAZZY RUNNER

Inspired both by traditional English methods and the energetic and vibrant patterns of Berber tribal rag rugs, with their areas of random mixed colours, this joyful runner incorporates all your family cast-offs, such as patterned socks, leggings and dyed and felted jumpers.

YOU WILL NEED:

- Pencil, coloured pencils, paper
- Indelible marker, chalk
- Ruler, tape measure
- 2 pieces of hessian, each 92 × 45 cm (36 × 18 in)
- Assorted durable fabrics
- Scissors
- Fabric gauge
- Large transparent plastic bags
- Spring-clip hook
- Assorted needles, cotton, woollen yarn
- Latex adhesive, spreader
- Dyed Merino fleece
- Woven and knitted woollens, cut into strips
- Felting needle, size 36/38
- Felting sponge
- Old tights
- Pins

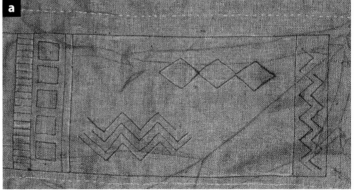

1 If necessary, draw the design on a large sheet of paper first, filling the different areas with colour as a reference.

2 Hemming along both sides of one piece of hessian, redraw the design within a 92 × 38 cm (36 × 15 in) rectangle using your chalk and then your indelible marker (**a**).

3 Using scissors and a fabric gauge when helpful, cut a variety of fabrics into prodding-sized pieces (see Preparation, page 38). Sort them into colours and tones, filling one transparent bag with a variety of pale neutral shades. Other bags should be filled with different colours, and their various tones, for the other shapes (**b**).

4 Begin working with the spring-clip hook (see Techniques, page 42) by pulling a few different fabric pieces through appropriate areas of the design, as colour reminders (**c**). Continue filling in the shapes marked out on the hessian, ensuring that your spacing creates the desired thickness of pile. Create an adaptation of the 'mizzy-mazzy' effect, both in the neutral background and also within several shapes, by mixing the tones of each colour.

5 Once the rug is completed, place the other piece of hessian on top of the runner's reverse, mark its outer shape and cut around it, leaving a reasonable excess all the way round for turning under and hemming.

6 Setting this aside, turn under 4 cm (1½ in) surplus hessian all the way around the runner, mitring the corners and concealing any excess. Spread the reverse and mitres with a thin layer of latex, and allow it to dry for a few minutes. Repeat the process, again allowing drying time.

7 Position the hemmed hessian lining on the reverse of the runner, and press the entire surface areas together. Allow this to dry overnight.

8 Adjust and trim the rug pile on the front surface where necessary, leaving it shaggier in some areas, slightly bevelling the sides, and clarifying the design's shapes (**d**).

9 Make approximately sixteen felted balls in different sizes and colours. A combination of methods can be used, including wet-felting (Embellishment, page 52 and follow Step 12 in the Lady tea cosy instructions on page 100).

10 Attach them, side by side, to each end of the runner's base cloth, using a crewel needle and a double length of woollen yarn (**e**).

OVAL RAG RUNNER

A colourful, hard-wearing mat with a braided surface created by the spider tool, perfect for using up all those fabric scraps and outgrown T-shirts and tights.

YOU WILL NEED:

- Hessian, 100 × 60 cm (39 × 24 in)
- Wooden metre stick ruler
- Chalk, indelible marker
- 60 cm (24 in) square wooden mat-making frame
- Drawing pins
- Assorted smooth, stretchy fabrics
- Scissors
- Spider tool
- Latex adhesive, spreader
- Needle, thread
- Suitable lining fabric

1 On your piece of hessian, with the aid of your metre ruler, draft a long oval shape measuring 40 × 75 cm (16 × 30 in) in chalk, and then go over this with an indelible marker (**a**).

2 It will be easier to use the spider tool on hessian that has been stretched taut. Pin the hessian onto a suitable sturdy frame to expose the initial area to be worked.

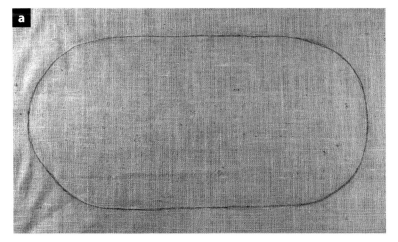

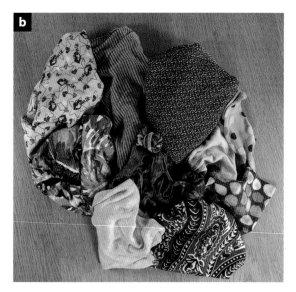

3 Having selected a range of suitable fabrics with an attractive varied palette, cut out a good amount of long fabric strips, approximately 1.2 cm (½ in) wide (**b**).

4 Thread your spider tool with a fabric strip, with the longer length of the fabric pushed through the hole near the handle and along the metal concave inner surface of the tool, so that a short end of the fabric is protruding beyond the tool's point (**c**).

5 Begin working along the drawn outline on the hessian so that your work will progress in rows, from the outer edge inwards. Holding your hook underneath the hessian, point the tip through to the top surface, allowing the visible fabric strip along the convex side of the tool to be looped around the point, aided by the thumb and index finger of your spare hand (**d**).

6 Draw the spider tool back downwards and out of the hessian, and leaving a small space, reinsert it, repeating the first step (**e**). Once the spider tool is pushed right through to the front surface, the first link of your chain will be apparent.

7   Continue this process, pushing each
    new loop through the previous one,
    and gently tugging on your loop of
    fabric each time so that a firm, secure
    row of chain links is created (**f**).

8   Once a strip of fabric has been
    finished, the end should be left
    underneath and a new strip begun
    in the same way, inserting it first into
    the same space as the end of the last
    strip. This will leave two ends of fabric
    next to each other (**g**).

9   If you don't have enough of one
    particular fabric to complete the row,
    part of the charm of the technique is
    to mix and match the patterns and
    colours (**h**).

10 Once you have completed one part
    of the rug, unpin it from your frame
    and readjust the work, pinning it
    to expose the last section to be
    worked (**i**).

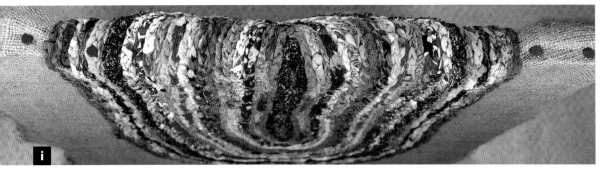

11 Your reverse side will consist of connected running stitches, with the fabric strip ends being left on this side. These can be trimmed neatly (**j**).

12 Once the rug is completed and you are satisfied with the overall shape, cut around the outer surface, leaving a hessian overlap of 5 cm (2 in) for turning under. Leaving the outer 5 mm (¼ in) edge free, the reverse surface can then be spread with latex (**k**).

13 Once the latex is dry, fold the overlap underneath. Stitch carefully, working from the front surface (**l**), to ensure that no chain links are disturbed or excess hessian is showing.

14 The lining fabric should be cut to the same shape as the rug, with an excess of up to 5 cm (2 in) for turning under. Pin it in place and neatly hem to finish (**m**).

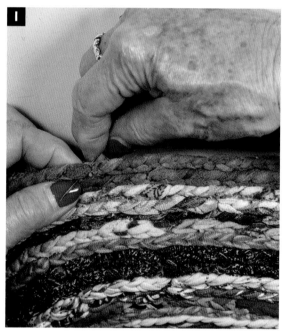

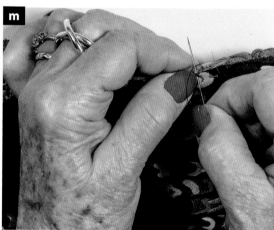

SPOTTY LOVEBIRD CUSHION

A comfy cushion for the playroom floor or your living room sofa, this chirpy bird should make you feel like spring has sprung! The design could also be framed for a wall piece.

YOU WILL NEED:

- Indelible marker
- Tracing paper
- Coloured pencils, transfer pencil, ruler
- Pressing cloth, iron
- Frame
- Hessian to fit
- Drawing pins or staple gun and staples
- Assorted colourful fabrics, including net, blanket wool, velvet and T-shirt cotton, cut into long strips, 1 cm (½ in) wide
- Rug hook
- Novelty and textured yarns
- Scissors
- Needles, sewing threads, dressmaker's pins
- 9 shisha mirrors, button
- Flexible wire or scoobies
- Felting needle, size 36/38
- Dyed fleece: red, yellow, orange and green
- Felting sponge
- Latex adhesive, spreader
- Lining material, 66 cm (26 in) square
- Colour co-ordinated canvas, 66 cm (26 in) square
- Velcro sew-on hook and loop tape, 38 cm (15 in)
- Polyester-filled cushion pad, 56 cm (22 in)

1 Follow Step 1 of the Hooked and braided rug instructions on page 92.

2 Attach the hessian tightly onto your frame, ensuring that the 56 cm (22 in) square design is positioned centrally and not distorted.

3 Using four similarly toned fabrics, start to hook the squares along each side of the design with alternating colours (**a**), roughly matching opposite sides.

4 When hooking the bird's head, leave small spaces for the mirrors and eye to be stitched, and also for the fleece-sculpted areas (**b**).

5 This area can be worked in a patterned fabric, with thick woollen yarn to chain hook a few lines within the hooked loops, to emphasise the bird's shape (see Techniques, page 43).

6 Hook the outlines of the scalloped wings with novelty yarns (**c**).

7 Within the tail strip, create additional stripes with a number of raised wrapped wire loops (see Techniques, page 43) (**d**), securing them through the hooking to the reverse of the design.

8 With a length of wire or scoobie, create the green flower stem similarly, determining its shape by couching it over the hooked area (**e**). Other stems can be hooked in green fabric, the loops being sheared.

9 Hook the background area within the border in a mainly lateral direction, to give the design some further contrast. Leave spaces for the felt heart and leaves to be applied.

10 Shear the loops of the hooked pink flower above the bird to create textural interest (**f**).

11 Use woollen blanket fabrics to hook both the bird's legs and the flower in the bottom right of the design, carving and sculpting both afterwards (**g**) (see Techniques, page 43). With the same treatment, use fleece strips for hooking the bulbous flower head (**h**).

12 Differ your hooking height in parts of the other flower, shearing some of the longer loops.

13 With a felting needle, dyed fleece and sponge (see Techniques, page 49) create the heart, flower, leaves and fleece-sculpted centres. Decorate the leaves with stitched woollen detail. Stitch them all in place, shaping the heart by sewing down its centre tightly (**i**).

14 Remove the design from your frame, trimming the overlapping hessian to 5 cm (2 in) around the design and folding it to the back. Stitch this in place from the front, concealing any exposed hessian. Tidy excess loose threads and scoobies on the reverse side.

15 Apply latex thinly to the reverse surface, allowing it to dry overnight. Turning the edges of all four sides underneath, attach lining fabric using ladder stitch (**j**).

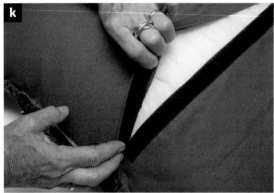

16 With a sturdy canvas fabric, cut two pieces for the cushion back, measuring 32.5 × 53 cm (13 × 21 in) and 25 × 53 cm (10 × 21 in), plus extra for attaching Velcro and seam allowances. After the edges have been hemmed, machine stitch a 45 cm (18 in) length of the hooked surface of Velcro along the inside of the larger piece of fabric, and the looped length to the outside of the smaller piece, ensuring that they correspond (**k**).

17 After turning in the edges along all sides, ladder stitch the smaller panel, then the larger one, in place, to form the back of the cushion. Insert the cushion pad, closing the fastening.

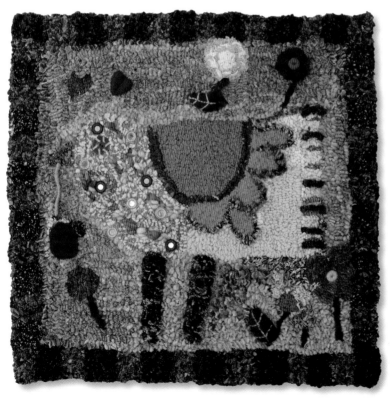

STITCHED SCRIBBLES WALL HANGING

Incorporating simple calligraphic patterns and a variety of tools and techniques to provide a range of textures and marks, this joyous wall hanging can be as colourful as you choose to make it. Feel free to change the sequence of the tools and techniques you use for each line to create your own unique design.

YOU WILL NEED:

- 280g- (10 oz-) weight hessian, 90 cm (1 yd)
- Mat-making frame
- Chalk, indelible marker
- Drawing pins and hammer, or staple gun and staples
- Scissors, embroidery scissors
- 4 different patterned fabrics, cut into long 13 mm- (½ in-) wide strips
- Needles, linen thread
- Rug hook
- Scoobies or flexible wire
- Assorted yarns in different colours and textures
- Rug wool
- Spider tool
- Oxford regular punch needle, size 10
- 8 mm- (⅓ in-) wide rubber-coated garden wire, 15 cm (6 in) length
- Handful of dyed merino fleece
- Felting needle, size 36/38
- Felting sponge
- Recycled sari silk yarn, fine mohair
- Latch hook
- Buttons
- PET plastic sequins
- Interlining fabric, 30 × 38 cm (12 × 15 in)
- Hessian for lining, 33 × 40 cm (13 × 16 in)
- Dowel rod, ribbon, or hanger of your choice, 38 cm (15 in) length

1 Attach the hessian onto your frame, keeping it taut. Mark out a 30 × 38 cm (12 × 15 in) rectangle. If preferred, first 'scribble' your design within the rectangle with chalk, and when satisfied, go over your lines with an indelible marker (**a**).

2 Thread a long strip of one of your fabrics onto a wide-eyed needle and make small lateral stitches along three sides of the rectangle outline (**b**), keeping the base free.

3 With a different fabric, hook the first line of your design (**c**), leaving a small part of it to be completed by wrapping a co-ordinating woollen yarn around a double length of scoobie or flexible wire (**d**) (see Techniques, page 43). Couch this in place with the same yarn at 13 mm (½ in) intervals.

4 Use the spider tool to work the braided surface on the next line of your design, using a different fabric (**e**). You can also achieve this by chain hooking (see Techniques, page 43) if you don't have this tool.

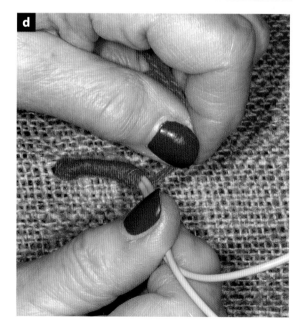

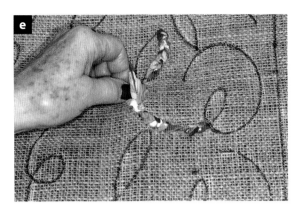

5 Wrap a single scoobie or wire with thread, and once you have achieved the required length to cover the drafted line, couch this in place as before at 13 mm (½ in) intervals, leaving a small section of the line to be completed (**f**).

6 Wrap your rubber-coated garden wire with a handful of matching toned merino fleece, creating a covered flexible felt tube, working on your felting sponge with your felting needle (**g**) (see Techniques, page 49). Once you are satisfied with the shape, carefully stitch this into place with a fine needle and matching thread.

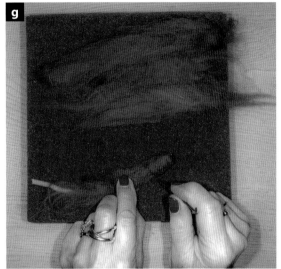

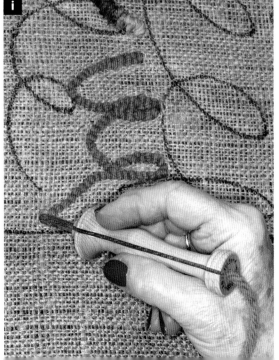

7 Hook most of the shape on the fourth line with your rug hook in your remaining fabric choice (**h**).

8 Using your punch needle and rug wool, work the remaining shape on that line, creating the flat stitch on the front surface (**i**).

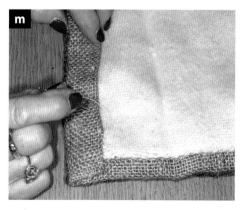

9 With a variety of threads, including recycled sari silk and fine mohair, create a row of fringe with your latch hook (**j**), along the base outline of the design.

10 Stitch your buttons along the top of the fringe at intervals (**k**).

11 Embellishments, such as PET plastic sequins (see Supplies and resources, page 154) can be attached to some of the threads for decorative effect (**l**).

12 Cut around the design, leaving a sufficient overlap in the hessian. Turning the work over, cover the reverse surface with your piece of interlining, and turning back the overlap, carefully stitch these two surfaces together. With an additional piece of hessian, back the work, ensuring that the stitched fabric edges remain exposed (**m**).

13 The wall hanging can be hung in different ways: using a dowel rod, or simply a cloth strip or ribbon hanger. This hanger has been fixed at the back through small loops of cloth that have been stitched at the top of each side, near the top of the work (**n**).

TOADSTOOL BROOCH

This needle-punched woollen woodland brooch is the perfect accessory, adorning a shirt or jumper on its own, or grouped together with other pins.

YOU WILL NEED:

- Small embroidery hoop, 11 cm (4½ in) diameter
- Linen punch needle foundation fabric, 18 cm (7 in) square
- Chalk, fine indelible pen, pencil
- Embroidery scissors
- Lavor punch needle, needle threader
- Needle, thread
- Crewel or tapestry wools
- Latex, fine spreader or cocktail stick
- Tracing paper
- Pins
- Small piece of felt
- Brooch pin

1 Either freehand or with the aid of a card template, draw the toadstool shape, approximately 7 × 8 cm (2¾ × 3¼ in), onto your piece of linen backing cloth with chalk and then go over it with a fine marker pen (**a**). This will be the side you work on, but it will become the reverse side of the work.

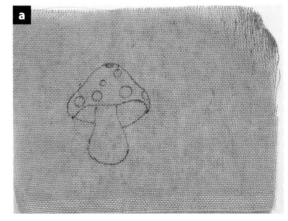

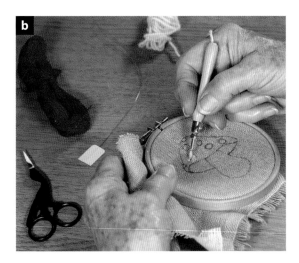

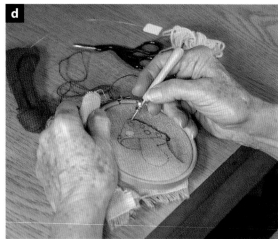

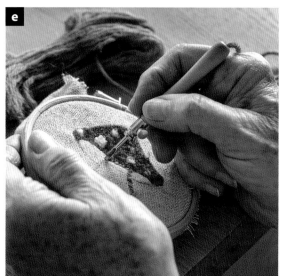

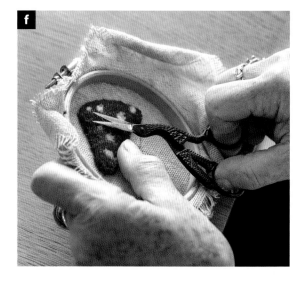

2 Insert the linen into your embroidery hoop, keeping the design in the centre and the fabric taut (**b**).

3 Using your threader, thread your punch needle with red yarn. Adjust the protruding length of your needle to approximately 1.5 cm (½ in), or according to the desired pile height on the other side (**c**).

4 Start needle punching around the outline of the toadstool's shape, creating only one or two threads in the linen as your spacing so that it is densely packed (**d**). Gradually fill in the shape, alternating with working the small spots so that these are given clarity (**e**). When you turn the work over, the surface should be a relatively dense pile (**f**).

5 Needle punch the stalk area in a light brown yarn, creating a similar pile height and surface to the upper part.

6 Work the underside of the toadstool on both sides of the stalk in a slightly lower, flatter pile, using a slightly darker tone of red yarn.

7 Perfect the white circles, and trim away any loose threads with your embroidery scissors. When you are satisfied with the finished shape, release the fabric from the frame (**g**).

8 Cut carefully around the toadstool shape with your embroidery scissors, leaving a small overlap, and snipping in towards the outer edge of the toadstool at a few corners (**h**).

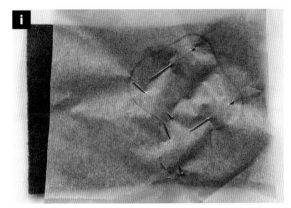

9 Turning the work over, carefully fold the overlapping linen inwards. Thinly apply latex adhesive with a fine spreader or cocktail stick, pressing all overlapping linen to the reverse surface of the work

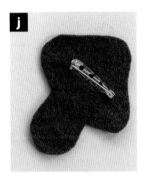

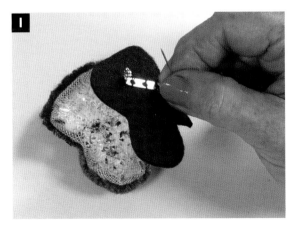

10 Trace the reverse of the toadstool's outline and pin the tracing paper onto a piece of felt (**i**).

11 Cut the shape out and stitch a brooch pin onto its centre (**j**).

12 Spread the toadstool's reverse surface with latex (**k**).

13 Carefully attach the felt back onto the toadstool's reverse (**l**). Leave to dry.

TOOTH FAIRY PILLOW

Which child, on losing a tooth, would not be happy to hang this in their bedroom, or place it by their pillow to await a visit from the tooth fairy?

YOU WILL NEED:

- Tracing paper
- Pencil, transfer pencil
- Drawing pins or staple gun and staples
- Frame
- Hessian, to fit
- Drawing pins or staple gun and staples
- Iron, pressing cloth
- Indelible marker
- Assorted fabrics, including gold and silver, cut into fine 5 mm (¼ in) strips
- Rug hook
- Assorted braids and trims, including net, sequins and rickrack
- Scissors
- Needles, threads
- Tiny coloured glass beads, silver bead or metallic coin
- Woollen fabric, 25 × 30 cm (10 × 12 in)
- Latex adhesive, spreader
- Wadding (batting)
- Lining fabric, 25 × 30 cm (10 × 12 in)
- Pink braided piping cord, 109 cm (43 in) length

1 Follow Step 1 of the hooked and braided rug instructions on page 92, placing the design within an outer measurement of 24 × 28 cm (9½ × 11 in) (**a**). Attach this to your frame, ensuring that the design is placed centrally and does not distort when stretched.

2 Use a blend of pink fabrics for hooking the tooth fairy's dress (**b**), and flesh tones for her face and arms.

3 Stitch either gathered net or net braid to decorate the bottom of the fairy's dress (**c**), and shear the loops of her wings once they have been hooked in a printed nylon (**d**).

4 Hook the fairy's hair finely in a range of yellow and ochre tones, and her crown and shoes in gold fabrics.

5 Fill in the details of the fairy's face carefully, matching slightly darker tones for the nose and face outline. With a fine pair of scissors, trim and adjust any details.

6 Use a soft but sturdy lilac fabric for the hooked even rows of background, ensuring that the fairy's shape is maintained.

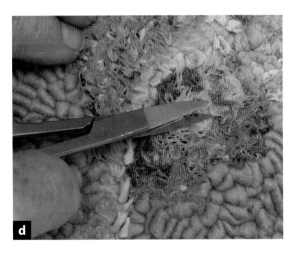

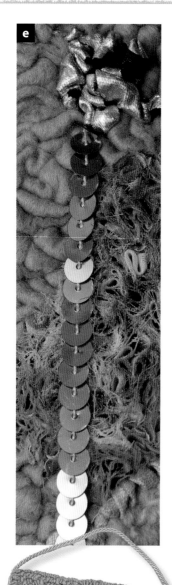

7   Hook a silver star, and complete the wand by using a 10 cm (4 in) strip of sequinned braid (**e**), secured on the reverse side at each end.

8   Thread tiny beads for the fairy's necklace (**f**), securing again on the reverse, and stitch a bead or coin 'jewel' into place on her hand.

9   Make a small pocket for the dress in contrasting fabric, folding the excess fabric behind, and embellishing with a tooth shape cut from white fabric (**g**). Embellish further with a strip of rickrack braid. Stitch the pocket into position on the hooked dress, leaving the top open for future tooth and coin deposits!

10 Leaving a hessian overlap of 2.5 cm (1 in) around the design, repeat Steps 14 and 15 of the Spotty lovebird cushion instructions on page 112, as applicable.

11 Placing wadding between, and turning the excess fabric behind, stitch the lining fabric to the hessian just within the outer edge of the design.

12 Allowing sufficient space for hanging the pillow, stitch the piping cord around three sides between the lining and the hooked design (**h**), leaving the top edge unpiped (**i**).

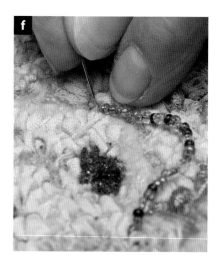

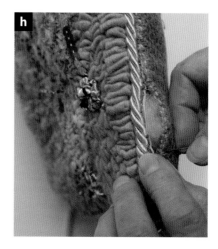

BIRDIE TOTE BAG

This bag makes an ideal child's shopper or a sleepover bag for packing pyjamas. However, it can also be scaled up for a larger tote bag. Because the bag is already made up, and you are hooking onto a relatively rigid background, it can be worked freely on your lap, without a frame. Use smooth and stretchy fabrics for hooking.

YOU WILL NEED:

- Hessian tote bag (see Supplies and resources, page 154)
- Indelible marker
- Card, transfer pencil or tracing paper (optional)
- Patterned and plain stretchy and woollen fabrics, cut into 1.5 cm- (½ in-) wide strips
- Rug hook
- Sparkly patterned Lycra
- Scissors
- Bodkin, needles, thread
- Curtain ring
- Gold or metallic thread
- Blue button
- 3 coloured yarns
- Latex adhesive, spreader

1 Either draw the design onto the bag freehand or make templates of the bird and flower head and draw around them with a marker, placing the bird centrally on the bag front (**a**). Draw the remaining details, including the lettering, freehand or use a transfer pencil and tracing paper, as instructed in the Christmas stocking (see page 67) and other projects.

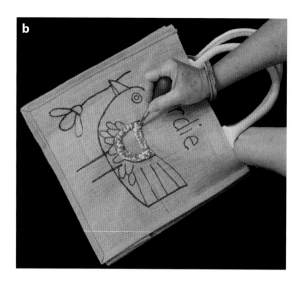

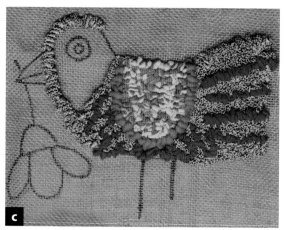

2 Use strips of patterned stretchy fabric to hook the 'saddle' of the bird, working it concentrically from the outline inwards (**b**). Outline this shape with one row hooked in a darker plain fabric.

3 Hook the outlined details of the bird in a bright, plain fabric to stand out (**c**).

4 Hook the remainder of the bird's body, around and within these details, in a sparkly patterned Lycra, to give the design some shimmer and glitz. Manipulate the details of the bird carefully into place as you proceed with the hooking.

5 The beak should be hooked using two tones of woollen fabric. Once completed, the beak's loops can be sheared to give it a contrasting texture (**d**).

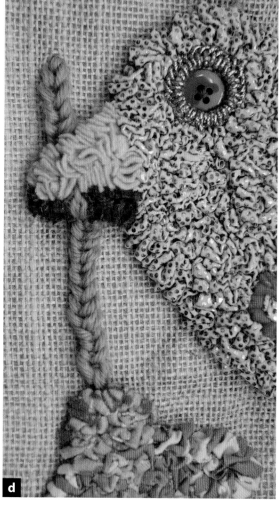

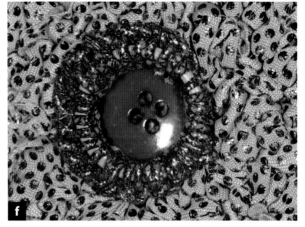

6   Make a lark's head knot around a curtain ring, using strong metallic thread (**e**). Continue making knots until the ring is covered, tucking in the thread ends with a needle to secure. Stitch the button in place, and laying the gold ring over this, stitch it to complete the eye (**f**).

7   Chain hook the lettering, flower stem and bird's legs (**g**) (see Techniques, page 43). Use a different colour and texture of yarn for each of these sections.

8   Trimming any loose ends, spread a thin layer of latex over the reverse of the hooked area of the bag. Stand the bag on its rectangular base and allow to dry overnight.

8 COMMUNITY PROJECTS

As practised historically by families and neighbours on both sides of the Atlantic, larger-scale rag-rug projects can be ideally suited to a collaborative effort within a broad range of circumstances and settings. Perhaps the affordability, relative ease and rapid achievement level of the craft all help to make the medium attractive and accessible as a group venture.

Most larger rug frames will accommodate six people, seated alongside and opposite each other, simultaneously working on a particular piece of work. This sort of group effort is usually very sociable and democratic, as well as having its obvious creative benefits. Perhaps because the hands are occupied with soothing and repetitive techniques, intimate conversation and the exchange of ideas are permitted and encouraged. In such a setting, I have known health and wellbeing information to be imparted, delicious recipes described and noted, and in the most natural and unselfconscious manner, counselling and support be both given and received.

Collaborative rag-rug projects can suit various stages of the school environment, where the end result might include the creation of a textile wall hanging to enhance a focal interior space within the building. Even the initial task of sourcing and sorting fabrics, which can involve many members of the school, can produce feelings of ownership and inclusion in the work by the pupils.

For primary-school ages, the medium can be an ideal way of addressing and including a broad range of cross-curricular themes. Aspects of literacy and science, such as the development and enrichment of vocabulary and descriptive language, plant and animal life, as well as design and technology, can be incorporated, while introducing the concept and handling of new tools, and the distinctions between natural and synthetic fibres.

At the other end of the spectrum, the medium often has significance for elderly people, who may indeed have memories of rag rugs and their tools, and the accompanying songs and stories, left over from childhood. The process of making a rag rug can provide a valuable parallel for, and access to, reminiscence work. In some parts of the country, where older volunteers provide support in schools, an intergenerational project can be very effective in building and enriching those special relationships.

Ways of working sometimes will depend upon the age and size of a group,

and their ideas about the design of the final piece. There are situations where it might be more appropriate for individuals to work on their own separate textiles on smaller frames. These could ultimately be stitched and joined together, contributing to the whole design. Having a larger adult group than can be accommodated at the rug frame is not necessarily problematic, since some people are willing to switch their roles from session to session, or simply happy to be part of the group socially, while cutting up fabrics or making the tea.

Making a rag rug might provide a focus for issue-based work, where a group wish to formulate and express certain ideas and concerns. The process, appropriate for addressing issues of conflict resolution and encouraging interfaith dialogue, is also suited to many health-related situations, including hospital and health centre waiting areas and occupational therapy departments. Since it is such a tactile medium, it also lends itself well to working with partially sighted people. The prodding technique, particularly, can effectively be used when working with individuals with learning disabilities. The work is stabilised on a rug frame, leaving both hands free to master the motion. Being able to make choices from a broad colour range of fabrics, and feeling their different weights and textures, is a vital part of the activity.

In primary-school projects, selecting predominantly smooth, stretchy, manageable fabrics, possibly sourced from T-shirts, leggings, knitwear and pyjamas, as well as providing an exciting vibrant palette, will be vital in making the task more enjoyable. The prodding technique is more suited to younger children, whereas those aged eight and over will usually master hooking.

As well as children's fiction, poems bearing strong visual imagery, such as those of Ted Hughes, Edward Lear and the cautionary verses of Hilaire Belloc, will lend themselves well to children's illustrations, and their subsequent translation into the medium, using both hooked and prodding techniques. Looking at

Above left: 'Mats for the Millennium' community textile project. Lynne Stein with Creative Minds, Eccleston, Lancashire, 1999. © Lynne Stein

Above: 'Everyone Smiles in the Same Language' interfaith textile project, Lynne Stein, 2011 onwards. DVI children's dental clinic, Jerusalem. © Lynne Stein

Risley Moss Nature Reserve, Warrington. Lynne Stein with Gorse Covert Primary School, 1997.
© Lynne Stein

the work of artists such as Clarice Cliff, Matisse and Hundertwasser, and their use of pattern, can provide a focus for individual hooked panels with eight- to eleven-year-olds. Drawing and painting self-portraits and those of classmates, in the styles of Picasso or the Old Masters, and observing facial expressions, colour and costume, can also be a good starting point for fabric work. For older design and technology pupils, a project could be based on the theme of underwater life, incorporating the preliminary processes of tie-dye, batik and silk painting, in preparation for making hooked panels for cushions or bags.

Within a busy waiting area of a children's clinic, the invitation to partic-ipate in creating a group 'work of art' which will eventually brighten up an otherwise dismal and unwelcoming treatment space can alleviate anxiety and boredom while teaching a child exciting new skills. Possible themes are endless, ranging from the depiction of myths and fables, and cartoon characters, to using children's thoughts and feelings about visits to the doctor or dentist as the inspi-ration for primary artwork for a collaborative wall hanging.

Children's libraries also provide an opportunity to enhance the space with a vibrant and colourful rag rug. A mat, which is made for the children to sit on at story time, could also be hung on the wall for all to see. A library or public building might be just the place to display the visual storytelling of a local historical event, or the celebration of a significant centenary. The preliminary research for such a work can occupy all members of the group, as can decision making about the eventual design.

Much that has been said about community involvement using handhooking and tufting techniques can apply to other textile processes, such as the making of a large collaborative latch-hooked textile or a piece worked using the punch needle. Although the distinct advantages of employing rag-rug tools and techniques are the emphasis upon recycling and consequent access to a wide fabric selection, the tools for these other predominantly yarn-based crafts are relatively inexpensive. As well as being able to purchase and include a broad range and spectrum of fibres and threads, charity shop finds and access to manufacturers' surplus and recycled yarns are also possible.

Since latch hooking is predominantly worked on a relatively rigid canvas, no frame is necessary, and the work can simply be rolled up between sessions. If using the punch needle technique or the spider tool, an appropriate choice of backing cloth would be stretched on a frame in much the same way as for a rag-rug project. The flat stitch surface of needle punch would need to be simultaneously worked by all participants, with the ability to view both sides as the work progresses. However, in some cases, it might be appropriate for elements of the work to be done on individual frames and eventually put together as one entire piece.

The latch-hook method is well-suited to creating both distinct, bold shapes and for depicting more complex painterly images. It is possible to create highly textured, tactile and undulating surfaces, containing both fringed and sculptural elements. There is plenty of scope for combining several techniques, and for incorporating other methods such as coiling, wrapping, felting, crochet and stitch, as well as final embellishment with a variety of artefacts to enhance the work. Constructing these additional elements also offers the opportunity for involving an increased number of participants in a collaborative project.

Concerned with matters of thrift and ecology, and no doubt inspired by the work of several leading practitioners of their craft, darning and 'visible mending' have recently gained popularity and enjoyed something of a renaissance. Looking forward optimistically to a Covid-free future, and longing for a return to experiencing the combination of camaraderie and craft, there is already increasing evidence of a resurgence in clothing 'repair cafés', 'make-do-and-mend' groups and collaborative textile initiatives across Britain.

The Birds and the Bees and the Flowers and the Trees. Knutsford community latch-hook project, 2022.
© Lynne Stein

9 GALLERY

The following examples will, I hope, indicate the vast potential for experimentation, self-expression and creativity using hooking, prodding, punching and tufting techniques. Whether their emphasis is upon creating sculptural relief surfaces or abstract or detailed graphic imagery, or making functional, decorative, traditional or contemporary works addressing personal or conceptual themes, there is visible evidence in the work of different artists and makers – both past and present – of an exciting and inspiring diversity of approaches.

Above: *Two Lions*. Joan Moshimer, 1997. 1.24 × 1.75 m (49 × 69 in). 100 per cent wool. Hand-dyed. One of America's best-known and respected designers, makers and teachers of rug hooking. Having designed over 400 in her lifetime, this was the last rug Joan completed before her death in 2000. Picture credit: Jesse Dupree. © Warren Roos

Above: *Girl with Bird Cage and Girl with Flowers.* Evelyn Ackerman, designed 1959 in both warm and cool colourways. 40.6 × 121.9 cm (16 × 48 in). Combining fine art, craft and industry to produce decorative, affordable objects was central to Evelyn and Jerome Ackerman's fifty-year creative output. Evelyn's textiles were just one element of their successful design practice, which included ceramics, mosaics, tapestries, hardware and woodcarvings, all characteristic of the best of California mid-century modernism. Evelyn's hand-hooked designs display a carefully chosen palette, a keen eye for pattern and her fondness for the tactile nature of the medium. © 2021 by ERA Industries/Evelyn Ackerman. Reproduced by permission of Ackerman Modern. All rights reserved.

Above: *Coral Garden.* Vanessa Barragão, 2018. Using a mixture of crochet, latch hook, tufting and hand-carving, Vanessa's work has been inspired largely by her grandmothers and their use of traditional textile techniques. © Studio Vanessa Barragão Textile Art & Design Studio

Left: *Face.* Traute Ishida, 1969. 183 × 244 cm (6 × 8 ft), 2.5 cm (1 in) pile. Latch hook. All wool. The carefully balanced composition and curved shape of the piece are typical of the artist's work of this time. © Susumu Ishida

Below: *Luna.* Anna Perach, 2021. Tufted yarn, artificial hair, wooden stand. Anna's main medium of work is wearable sculpture and performance. © Paul Chappalier

Above: *Santa Fe.* Micah Clasper-Torch, 2018. Punch needle coat. Wool, yarn, monks cloth. With a BFA in Fashion Design, Micah brings her combined knowledge and experience of fashion, art and design to her craft. © Davy Kesey

Right: *The Inside and Outside Are One.* Prunella Bramwell-Davies, 2008. 51 × 61 cm (20 × 24 in). Hooked cotton and mixed fibres. Shading and volume are successfully achieved by the compact hooking and closely blended fabric tones. © Ian Hessenberg

Left: *Fuzzy-7.* Alfhild Sarah Külper, 2020. 1.4 × 1.4 m (55 × 55 in). Gun-tufted. Largely recycled yarns. Much of Alfie's work focuses on abstract memories and emotional interpretations of the beings around her.
© Arnhout Hulskamp

Below: *Listen Rug.* Barbara Klunder, 1998. 66 × 114 cm (26 × 45 in). Strips of hooking material include a variety of fabrics, from ribbons and T-shirts to ball gowns, in order to achieve her subtle colour blends and clarity of form.
© Jeremy Jones

Above: *Mischievous Cat*. Brandon Mably, 86 × 104 cm (34 × 41 in). Brandon loves searching for fabrics at charity shops and car-boot sales. Hooked loosely, the design and palette for this beautiful rug enhance the artefacts and furnishings within its interior. Picture credit: The Kaffe Fassett Studio. Featured in *Glorious Interiors* (London: Ebury Press, 1995), © Brandon Mably

Right: *Cat*. Louisa Creed, 1990. 81 × 69 cm (32 × 27 in). Mixed recycled materials, giving the piece volume and detail in its clever use of tones and textures.
© John Worrallo

Above: *Beast.* Adeline Wang, 2020. 70 × 70 cm (24 × 24 in). Inspired to use the punch needle technique by social media, Adeline's bold, colourful graphic designs are informed by daily life. © Adeline Wang

Left: *Happy Dog.* Lewis Creed, 2009. 56 × 56 cm (22 × 22 in). Latch hook. Mixed recycled materials. The outlined simple motifs and restricted palette give the piece a joyous cartoon-like quality. © John Worrallo

Above: *Mair at Cylch Meithrin.* Anya Paintsil, 2020. 106.7 × 91.4 cm (42 × 36 in).
Acrylic, wool and synthetic hair on hessian. Anya's work is largely autobiographical,
frequently exploring race, identity and mental health issues. She uses a variety of
tools and techniques, including punch needle, latch hook, sewing needles and
various Afro hairstyling tools. Courtesy: Ed Cross Fine Art. © Anya Paintsil

Above: *Gossip.* Jennifer Manuell, 2006. 23 × 30 × 5 cm (9 × 12 × 2 in). A Canadian fourth-generation rug hooker, Jennifer combines predominantly space-dyed yarns and self-dyed woollen fabrics to create the rich flora and fauna designs in her handbags. © Sandra Stetler

Left: *Bird With Stripe Flowers.* Arounna Khounnoraj, 2020. 29 × 39 × 2.5 cm (11½ × 15½ × 1 in). Punch needle. Wool stretched on wood. © Arounna Khounnoraj

Right: Necklace. Jennifer Manuell, 2013. Handhooked. Fabric, beads. © Sandra Stetler

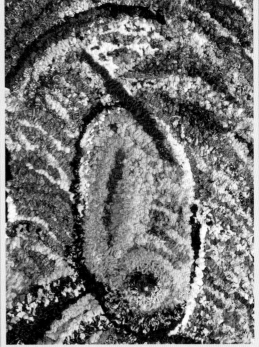

Above *Rug*. Jonathan Josefsson. 170 × 135 cm (67 × 53 in). Gun-tufted. Mixed fibres. Jonathan is also a graffiti artist, which clearly influences his textiles. © Jonathan Josefsson

Left: *Tufted No. 2*. Caroline Kaufman, 2019. 120 x 150 cm (4 x 5 ft). Hand-dyed, hand-spun wool, cotton and natural fibres. With a background in fashion and knitwear design, Caroline's bright geometric tufted creations function equally well when hung on the wall or as rugs on the floor. © Caroline Kaufman

Right: Untitled (detail). Lynne Stein. 2019. 1.45 × 1.12 m (57 × 44 in). Gun-tufted, needle felted. Mixed largely recycled fabrics and fibres, fleece. Courtesy of Bernard and Maralyn Roberts. © Lynne Stein

Left: *Squirrel.* Designed by Nathalie Lété, 2014. Handmade in Albania. 1.4 × 2 m (55 × 79 in). Pure wool woven, tufted, and embroidered tapestry rug. © Alain le Prince

Above: *P.J.B.* Lu Mason, 1995. 152 × 91 cm (5 × 3 ft). Wool on hessian, tweeds and brightly coloured fabrics. Inspired by 1950s fabrics and plates, African prints and 1920s and 1930s Russian painted china. © Lu Mason

Left: *Dancing at the Bus Stop.* Diane Cox, c. 2020. Handhooked, pencil rug hook. Mixed recycled fabrics. Storytelling and the narrative element have been very important in Diane's work. © Hugo Trevorrow

Right: *Ya ZaZa*. Hannah Epstein, 2018.
170 × 114 cm (67 × 45 in). Wool, acrylic,
polyester, burlap. Courtesy of Steve Turner
Gallery © Wild Don Lewis Photography

Below: *Fallen Fish of Mên a Tol*. Hollie
Palmer, 2020. 2.5 × 1.5 m (98½ × 59 in).
Punch needle. Largely recycled yarns.
Hollie's work is a reflection of her domestic
environment and the local Cornish
landscape. This large rug was inspired by
a walk with friends across Mên-an-Tol to
Zennor. © Hollie Palmer

Left: *You Only Come to Me Whilst I Fall*. Selby Hurst Inglefield, 2020. 100 × 80 cm (39½ × 31½ in). Needle punch. Wool on hessian. © Selby Hurst Inglefield

Right: *Dove and Dog Angel*. Sue Dove, 2018. 115 × 148 cm (45 × 58 in). Rug hooking. Recycled T-shirts, vintage fabrics, stitch. Based on the idea of herself and her dog as angels, Sue's vibrant work is a continuation of her collage, painting and embroidery, and celebrates many of the simple and joyous aspects of life. © Hugo Trevorrow

Left: Sofa bed. Ali Rhind, 2005. Using mainly woollen self-dyed blankets to prod boldly patterned fabric, perfectly suited to upholstery, this sofa bed was made for a caravan as part of the celebratory touring exhibition, 'Trailer Made', in collaboration with Designed & Made, Newcastle. © David Lawson

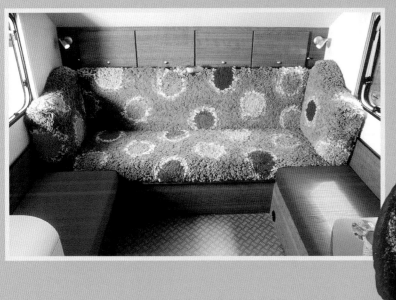

Right: *MeMe Mat*. Trish Little, 2000. 45 × 108 cm (18 × 43 in). Largely recycled assorted fabrics hooked into hessian. Trish's work, sometimes taking on a three-dimensional form, is often a passionate response to political issues and the wide-open spaces of the West Australian Goldfields area in which she lives. © Gary Blinco

Left: *Gratitude Dolls.* Trish Andersen, 2020. 30 × 45 × 13 cm (12 × 18 × 5 in). The 'dolls' were created at the beginning of lockdown. Trish uses a variety of single needle tufting guns, the repetitive and meditative nature of the process helping her to 'go to a soft world'. © Trish Andersen Courtesy of the Artist.

Below: *Mosaic.* Kaffe Fassett, 1993. 78 × 120 cm (31 × 47 in). Enjoying the vibrant colour and textural potential afforded by the medium, Kaffe's mosaic design is worked with a latch hook, using thrift shop fabrics. Comparable to traditional 'crazy paving' rag-rug patterns, the grey outlines in *Mosaic* give unity to the whole design. Picture credit: The Kaffe Fassett Studio. Featured in *Glorious Interiors.* (London: Ebury Press, 1995). © Kaffe Fassett

Below: *Mythological Beast.* Lynne
Stein, 1998. 56 × 56 cm (22 ×
22 in). Handhooked, wrapped wire,
stitched. Largely recycled fabrics and
embellishments. Inspired by fairy tales,
mythology and pantomime.
© Lynne Stein. Photo: Tamara Stein.

Above: *Cabbages and Lots of Flowers* (detail). Lynne Stein, 2009. 1.09 × 1.04 m
(43 × 41 in). Gun-tufted, needle felted, wrapped wire, stitched. Largely recycled
fabrics and fibres. Inspired by local allotments, their patterns and symmetry.
© Lynne Stein

Above: *Walking on Eggs.* Linda Rae
Coughlin, 2007. 38 × 43 cm (15 ×
17 in). Hooked, stitched, machine and
hand embroidered. Recycled fabrics,
linen foundation, threads, gold chain.
Linda combines rag-rug techniques,
embroidery and artefacts to make
political and personal gender
statements.
© Linda Rae Coughlin

Above: *Spot Rug.* Sara Worley, 2009. 90 × 60 cm (35 × 24 in). Hooked. Upcycled
mixed fabrics. The colours and bold contemporary graphic imagery in this rug
have a retro quality. © Sara Worley

Left: *Spotted Jug.* Sue Dove, 2010. 90 × 64 cm (35 × 25 in). Rug hooked. Recycled T-shirts, woollen yarn. © Hugo Trevorrow

Right: *Geraniums.* Emma Tennant, 2008. 61 × 89 cm (24 × 35 in). Also a painter and gardener, Emma's horticultural imagery and skilful juxtaposition of plain, tweed and twill fabrics give her rugs a distinctive appearance.
© Hermitage Rugs/Emma Tennant. Photo: Katie Pertwee

Right: *Tremble.* Traute Ishida, 1973. 200 × 224 cm. (78¾ × 88 in). Latch-hook, hand knotting and looping yarns. Acrylic fibres, nylon, wool. Traute was one of the most influential fibre artists of her era to use these techniques.
© Susumu Ishida

Left: *Under Watchful Eyes.* Rachelle Leblanc, 2011. 69 × 74 cm (27 × 29 in). Latch-hooked on linen backing cloth. Self-dyed 100 per cent wool and cashmere fabric strips. Rachelle's approach owes much to her passion for painting. Her themes are personal, often recapturing childhood memories.
© Rachelle Leblanc

Below: *In-Between-Selves.* Selby Hurst Inglefield, 2020. 2.5 × 1.5 m (98½ × 59 in). Wool, acrylic, beads, straw, buttons. Attracted and motivated by slower textile processes, Selby uses the Oxford size 10 punch needle and a vintage speed tufting machine in her work. © Selby Hurst Inglefield

Above: *Nursery Rug*. Lynne Stein, 2015. 84 × 56 cm (33 × 22 in). Handhooked, needle felted, chain hooked, stitched, embellished. Largely recycled fabrics, printed suede, fleece, feathers, buttons. Inspired by children's artwork after a trip to the zoo. © Lynne Stein

Right: Large cushion. Lynne Stein, 2020. 56 × 56 cm (22 × 22 in). Handhooked, prodded, wrapped wire, fleece and yarn sculpted, stitched, embellished. Largely recycled fabrics, yarns, pom-poms braids. © Lynne Stein

10 MUSEUM AND GALLERY COLLECTIONS

UK

Abbott Hall, Museum of Lakeland Life, Cumbria
American Museum, Bath
Beamish Open-Air Museum, Northumberland
Black Country Living Museum, West Midlands
The Bowes Museum, Barnard Castle
Cromer Museum, Norfolk
Eyemouth Museum, Whitby
Fashion and Textile Museum, London
Fife Folk Museum, Fife
Grace Darling Museum, Northumberland
Grosvenor Museum, Chester
Guernsey Folk Museum, Saumarez Park
Helmshore Mills Textile Museum, Lancashire
Highland Folk Museum, Inverness
Ironbridge Gorge Museum (Blists Hill), Shropshire
Kings Lynn Museum, Norfolk
Manx National Heritage Museum, Isle of Man
Museum of Carpet, Kidderminster
National Mining Museum of Scotland, Midlothian
National Waterways Museum, Ellesmere Port
Old Merchants House, Great Yarmouth
Rachel Kaye-Shuttleworth Collection, Gawthorpe
  Hall, Lancashire
Ryedale Folk Museum, North Yorkshire
Ruthin Craft Centre, North Wales
Scottish Fisheries Museum, Anstruther
Shipley Art Gallery, Gateshead
Stromness Museum, Orkney
Tullie House Museum, Carlisle
Ulster Folk and Transport Museum, Northern
  Ireland
Upper Dales Folk Museum, North Yorkshire
V&A Museum, London
Warner Textile Archive, Braintree, Essex
Welsh Folk Museum, Cardiff

Whitworth Art Gallery, Manchester
Woodhorn Colliery Museum, Northumberland
Yorkshire Museum of Farming, York

US

Billings Farm and Museum, Woodstock, Vermont
Cooper-Hewitt Smithsonian Design Museum, New
  York
Coutts Memorial Museum of Art, California
Creative Growth Art Center, California
De Young Museum, San Francisco, California
Henry Ford Museum, Michigan
Heritage Center of Lancaster County, Pennsylvania
The Historic Clothing and Textile Museum, Athens,
  Georgia
Huntington Museum of Art, West Virginia
Museum of American Folk Art, New York
Rhode Island School of Design Museum
Shaker Museum, New York
Shelburne Museum, Vermont
The Textile Museum, Washington D.C.
Wenham Historical Museum, Massachusetts

Canada

Art Gallery of Nova Scotia, Halifax
Canadian Craft Museum, Vancouver
Canadian Museum of Civilisation, Quebec
Chéticamp Hooked Rugs, Nova Scotia
McCord Museum of Canadian History, Montreal
Mississippi Valley Textile Museum, Almonte, Ontario
New Brunswick Museum, Newfoundland
North American Hooked Rug Museum, Nova Scotia
The Patricia Harris Gallery of Textiles and Costume
Royal Ontario Museum, Toronto
Textile Museum of Canada, Toronto

Australia

Ararat Gallery Textile Art Museum Australia, Victoria

Australian Museum of Clothing and Textiles, Maitland, New South Wales

Historic Houses Trust, New South Wales

Powerhouse Museum, Sydney

Tamworth Regional Gallery Textile Collection, New South Wales

New Zealand

Auckland Museum, Auckland

The Museum of New Zealand, Textiles and Dress Collection, Wellington

Further reading

Rug Hooking

Allan, Rosemary E., *From Rags to Riches: North Country Rag Rugs* (County Durham: Beamish North of England Open Air Museum, 2007)

Bawden, Juliet, *Rag Rug Inspirations* (London: Cassell, 1996)

Boswell, Thom (ed.), *The Rug Hook Book* (New York, USA: Sterling, 1992)

Davies, Ann, *How to Make Hand-Hooked Rag Rugs* (Tunbridge Wells: Search Press, 1996)

Davies, Ann, *Rag Rugs* (London: Letts, 1992)

Hinchcliffe, John and Jeffs, Angela, *Rugs from Rags* (London: Orbis Publishing, 1977)

Hubbard, Clare, *Making Rag Rugs* (Massachusetts, USA: Storey Books, 2002)

Kopp, Joel and Kate, *American Hooked and Sewn Rugs* (New York, USA: E.P. Dutton & Co. Inc., 1975)

Meany, Janet and Pfaff, Paula, *Rag Rug Handbook* (Colorado, USA: Interweave Press, 1996)

Pulido, Theresa, *Hook, Loop and Lock* (Ohio, USA: Krause Publications, 2009)

Reakes, Lizzie, *Ragwork* (London: Lorenz Books, 1996)

Reeves, Sue, *Country Rag Crafts* (Newton Abbot: David & Charles, 1996)

Tennant, Emma, *Rag Rugs of England and America* (London: Walker Books, 1992)

Vail, Juju, *Rag Rugs* (London: Apple, 1997)

Winthrop Kent, William, *The Hooked Rug* (New York, USA: Tudor Publishing, 1937)

Needle punching

Davidson, Lucy, *Punch Needle Embroidery for Beginners* (Tunbridge Wells: Search Press, 2020)

Khounnoraj, Arounna, *Punch Needle: Master the Art of Punch Needling Accessories for You and Your Home* (London: Quadrille, 2019)

Moore, Sara, *Punch Needle: 25 Quick and Easy Projects to Make* (London: The Guild of Master Craftsmen Publications, 2020)

Pearlman, Rose, *Modern Rug Hooking: 22 Punch Needle Projects for Crafting a Beautiful Home* (Colorado: Roost Books, 2019)

Rug making

Felcher, Cecelia, *The Complete Book of Rugmaking* (New York: Hawthorn Books Inc., 1975)

Znamierowski, Nell, *Rugmaking: A Complete Introduction to the Craft of Creative Rugmaking* (London: Pan Craft Books, 1972)

Latch hooking

Spiro, Lynda, *Latch-hooking Rugs* (London: A & C Black Publishers Ltd., 2008)

Locker hooking

Peguero, Leone, *Locker Hooking: An Introduction to the Craft* (London: Hodder & Stoughton, 1985)

Supplies and resources

UK

The Clever Baggers
www.thecleverbaggers.co.uk
(jute tote bags)

Cornish Stitch Designs
www.rugkit.co.uk
(wool, rug making, needlecrafts)

Cotton Patch
www.cottonpatch.co.uk
(textile supplies, textile hangers)

Daughter of a Shepherd
www.daughterofashepherd.com
(100% British woollen yarns)

Debbie Siniska
www.debbiesiniska.co.uk
(workshops, rug-making
  equipment)

DMC
www.dmc.com
(yarns and threads)

Etsy
www.etsy.com
(textile craft equipment)

Fred Aldous Ltd
www.fredaldous.co.uk
(textile and craft supplies)

George Weil
www.georgeweil.com
(textile craft equipment)

Hobbycraft
www.hobbycraft.co.uk
(textile craft equipment)

Jenni Stuart-Anderson
https://jenniragrugs.com
(workshops, rug-making
  equipment)

John Lewis
www.johnlewis.com
(textile craft equipment,
  haberdashery)

London Loop
www.loopknittingshop.com
(yarns and fibres, books and
  journals, classes)

Lynne Stein
www.lynnestein.com
(workshops, textile equipment)

Makings
www.makings.co.uk
(spider tool and rug-making
  supplies, accessories)

Neville Smith
https://rughook.com/pages/the-
  irish-hook-the-hartman-hook
(rug hooks and prodders)

Rag Art Studios
www.ragartstudios.com
(workshops, rug-making
  equipment)

Ragged Life
www.raggedlife.com
(rug-making equipment)

Rainbow Silks
www.rainbowsilks.co.uk
(workshops, textile craft
  equipment)

Rowan
www.knitrowan.com
(natural fibre yarns)

The Sustainable Sequin Company
www.thesustainablesequincom-
  pany.com
(large range of PET sequins)

Whole Punching
www.wholepunching.co.uk
(punch needle equipment)

Wingham Wool
www.winghamwoolwork.co.uk
(felting equipment, dyes)

Wool and the Gang
www.woolandthegang.com
(upcycled yarns)

US

Green Mountain Hooked Rugs
www.greenmountainhookedrugs.
  com
(rug-making equipment, dyes,
  classes)

Halycon Yarn
www.halcyonyarn.com
(rug-making and felting
  equipment, dyes, classes)

Morgan Hoops & Stands Inc.
www.nosliphoops.com
(hoop frames and stands)

The Oxford Company
www.amyoxford.com
(punch needle equipment, kits,
  classes, books)

Purl Soho
www.purlsoho.com
(fibre craft equipment, classes
  patterns, events)

Searsport Rug Hooking
www.searsportrughooking.com
(rug-making equipment, dyes)

Star Country Rug Hooking School
& Supply
www.iloverughooking.com
(rug-making equipment, dyes,
classes)

Tuft the World
www.tuftinggun.com
(tufting machines, frames, yarns,
backing cloth, starter kits)

Ultra Punch
ultrapunchneedle.com
(punch needle equipment)

W. Cushing & Co.
www.wcushing.com
(rug-making equipment, dyes)

Wandaworks
www.wandaworks.ca
(dyes, rug-making equipment,
classes)

Woolery
www.woolery.com
(fibre craft equipment)

Yankee Peddler Hooked Rugs
www.yankeepeddler.com
(rug-making equipment)

Yarn Tree
www.yarntree.com
(Q-snap and other frames)

Canada
Deanne Fitzpatrick Studio
www.hookingrugs.com
(rug-making equipment, classes)

The Knit Cafe
www.theknitcafetoronto.com
(fibre craft equipment, books,
classes)

Legacy Studio
www.legacystudio.ca
(rug-making and felting
equipment, dyes)

Punch Needle Rug Hooking
www.punchneedlerughooking.ca
(fibre craft equipment, classes)

Australia
Craft Folk
www.craftfolk.com.au
(fibre craft supplies, kits, classes)

Fibre Fusion
fibrefusion.com/au
(felting equipment)

Itchy Stitchy
www.itchystitchy.com.au
(textile craft supplies)

Studio Blue
www.ausrugcrafters.com
(rug-making equipment,
workshops)

The Studio Workshops
www.thestudioworkshops.com
(punch needle supplies)

New Zealand
All Things Effy
www.allthingseffy.com
(tufting machines, punch needles,
textile craft supplies, classes)

Guilds and societies

Association of Traditional
Hooking Artists
www.atharugs.com

Australian Rug Makers Guild
www.rughookingaustralia.com

Embroiders' Guild
www.embroiderersguild.com

Fiber Art Now
www.fiberartnow.net

The International Guild of
Handhooking Rugmakers
www.tighr.net

The Punch Needle Guild (online
group)
www.facebook.com/groups/
106783896681573

The Textile Society
www.textilesociety.org.uk

Textile Study Group
www.textilestudygroup.co.uk

Directories

The Rug Hookers Network
www.rughookersnetwork.com

tafalist.com
http://tafalist.blogspot.com

Journals and magazines

Hooking Matters
www.tighr.net/hooking-matters
(The International Guild of Handhooking
   Rugmakers' quarterly newsletter)

Rug Hooking Magazine
www.rughookingmagazine.com

Selvedge
www.selvedge.org

TextileArtist.org
www.textileartist.org
(online newsletter for textile and fibre artists)

The Wool Street Journal
www.woolstreetjournal.com

Social enterprises, co-operatives, collections

Berber Arts
www.berber-arts.com

Creative Growth Art Center
www.creativegrowth.org

Mielie
www.mielie.com

Rug Aid
www.rug-aid.org

The Rug Hook Project
www.rughookproject.com

Acknowledgements

Thank you to Susan James for commissioning the first edition of *Rag-Rug Creations: An Exploration of Colour and Surface*, first published by Bloomsbury in 2014, and to Agnes Upshall for seeing it through to publication. A big thank you to Jayne Parsons at Bloomsbury for her confidence and enthusiasm once again in encouraging the creation of an expanded edition of this book. Thanks also to Russell Butcher and Beth Dymond, for seeing the book through to its completion, to Jerry Goldie for an outstanding book design, and to Elle Chilvers and Krynn Hanold, my publicists at Bloomsbury/Herbert Press, who are always a joy to work with.

I am immensely grateful to Ali Rhind, who is partially responsible for 'getting me hooked' on rag-rug-making in the first place! I am indebted to all my generous contributors for allowing me to show their wonderful and varied work, and for being prepared to discuss their making processes and motivations.

I am additionally grateful to the following people, all of whom in different ways have given me their generous help: Charlotte Bell, Linda Berman, Gebhart Blazek, Lisette Bourgeois, Siegrun Brunt, Jesse Dupree, The Hidden Jem, Grace Flinn, Helen Flynn, Anne and Malvin Flynn, Melanie Gardner (Tullie House Museum and Art Gallery), Penny Godfrey, Jennifer Gordon (Scottish Fisheries Museum), Karen Griffiths, Iwona Hetherington (Powerhouse Museum), Sue Mosco, Maureen Morano, Jovan Nicholson, Joel Stein and Shelagh Wolfson.

Special thanks to both Laura Ackerman-Shaw and Annette Ishida for enabling the inclusion of the beautiful textile examples of both their mothers, Evelyn Ackerman and Traute Ishida. And to Mercedes Yau, Tamara Stein, Eloise Shneck and Lottie Powell, supermodels extraordinaires!

My appreciation to Sheila French, Julie Harrison, Sarah Hill, Suzy Powell, Lottie Powell, and Alison Reynolds, for their involvement in the community latch-hook project's early stages. And to my workshop students, past, present and future, I extend my appreciation for your continual willingness to 'play' and eagerness to learn new stuff. In turn, you have often been my teachers too, and many have become good friends. I hope this will continue to be so for many more years.

Last, but never least, my unfailing gratitude goes to my husband and photographic collaborator, Robbie Wolfson, for his extreme patience and encouragement, his unstinting love and support, and most importantly his excellent photographic skills and technical know-how throughout.

Index